Turning *the* World Upside Down

Paul and Privilege *with* These People Called Methodist

Aleze Fulbright, Michael Baughman, Ashley Boggan

Abingdon Press | Nashville

Turning the World Upside Down

Paul and Privilege with These People Called Methodist

Library of Congress Control Number: 2026939093

978-1-7910-4103-8

Continued on page iv.

Contents

Authors' Note v

Introduction vii

1. Saul's Privilege: Power, Perspective, and the Peril of Unexamined Advantage (Acts 7; 22) 1

2. The Call to Constant Conversion (Acts 9) 13

3. Genital Conference (Acts 15; 16:11-15) 29

4. When the World Calls Justice "Upside Down" (Acts 16:16-40) 45

5. Big Church Energy and Financial Privilege: Paul, Tentmaking, and the Freedom to Speak Truth (Acts 18; 24) 63

6. Paul's Witness in Athens, Part 1: Cultural Privilege and the Way of Wisdom (Acts 17:16-34) 75

7. Paul's Witness in Athens, Part 2: Curious Labor
(Acts 16:11-15; 17:16-34) 87

8. When Privilege Runs Out: Paul, the Hissy Fit,
and the Long Obedience of Staying (Acts 18; 22; 23) 99

9. A Time to Keep Silent (Acts 19:23-41; 20:7-12) 113

10. Claiming Sacred Citizenship:
Asserting Our Rights for the Sake of the Gospel
(Acts 22:25-28; 23:12-35) 129

Epilogue: There Is No Pretty Bow at the End of This Book 141

Notes 145

Continued from page ii.

Cover description: The title "Turning the World Upside Down" appears in large red text on a light background, featuring a small upside-down globe beneath the title. Subtitle reads "Paul and Privilege with These People Called Methodist," with author names Aleze Fulbright, Michael Baughman, and Ashley Boggan in white text on a blue banner at the bottom.

MANUFACTURED IN THE UNITED STATES OF AMERICA

Authors' Note

Reverend Raegan Gilliland once entertained a gathering of the North Texas Annual Conference of The United Methodist Church by leading a game she called "Lamentations or Taylor Swift Lyric." She brought two competitors to the stage—a biblical scholar and a pastor who also happened to parent a fourteen-year-old Taylor Swift fan. Gilliland put some lines on the screen, and the competitors had to correctly identify whether they were from a Taylor Swift song or from Lamentations.

It's way harder than you think.

Who is speaking at any given moment matters. A song of distress from Taylor Swift means something categorically different than grief from an Israelite poet living in exile. While the authors will certainly influence each other's words through conversation, editing, and shared exploration of the text, this book is clear about whose voice you are reading at any given moment. We do this for several reasons.

First, context matters. Mike is a White, well-educated, Jersey-Italian, fourth-generation Methodist pastor who has always struggled a bit with the church he loves. Aleze is a Black, well-educated, proud mother of a Black son, and a pastor in a dominant-culture denomination, who grew up in Tulsa, Oklahoma, served in North Texas, and now serves as a leader in The United Methodist Church in Indiana. While Mike and Aleze walk closely with family, friends, and congregants who identify on the LGBTQ+ spectrum, they are both cisgender and heterosexual. Their stories are distinct, as are their lenses through which they see the world. We want both authors to be seen and heard in the full context of who they are—and who they are not.

Second, representation matters. Far too often, White voices have claimed Black insight, wisdom, and pain. We have done our best to avoid that here. Far too often, people assume that statements about racial inequity are coming exclusively from Black voices.

Finally, integrity matters. We want to stand by our words, knowing they will be flawed and hopefully judged harshly by readers in decades to come for what we failed to see through the lens of the 2020s.

And then there's Ashley, who is not writing full chapters but tacks on some Wesleyana to the end of each chapter in an effort to relate an older celibate guy of the primitive church (Paul) with an older (White) celibate guy of the "wannabe" primitive church (John Wesley). Think of these as historical postcards reminding us that these people called Methodist have been turning the world upside down for a long time.

INTRODUCTION

Why I, and Other White Church Leaders, Need to Pay Way More Attention to the Book of Acts

Mike Baughman

More and more, I'm questioning the way I was taught to read the gospel—always looking for myself in the story. With a theater background, time spent with a Jesuit-influenced spiritual director, and enough empathy to make me cry my way through 98 percent of *This Is Us*, I'm pretty good at finding and amplifying points of connection between myself and just about any character. Lately, I've grown to worry that I may be doing this too much—that some of these stories are just not for me.

I used to think that I was, basically, the Syrophoenician/Canaanite woman (Matthew 15:21-28; Mark 7:24-30). My youngest daughter was born with congenital heart defects. I know what it is to put myself in the way of doctors, to put myself in the way of God, to demand that my daughter be healed. I would suffer any abuse for her healing. If my adult-sized heart could have fit in the tiny body of this human I had just met, it would have been hers. I preached her story like it was mine.

Years later, I invited a young, queer, Ethiopian immigrant woman to preach the same story. She named all the ways the Syrophoenician/ Canaanite woman—given her intersectional, oppressed identities—would have been dismissed as a woman, dismissed as a religious minority, dismissed as an outsider, dismissed as annoying by Jesus's disciples, and ultimately dismissed by Jesus's own label for her when he likens her to a little dog. She preached about what it is to place yourself in the way of authority and endure dehumanizing humiliation to get what you need for your family just to survive. I realized there is no way that I am the Syrophoenician woman. The number of boxes checked on my privilege card protects me from her experience and amplifies my voice so that I can never know what it means to fight like her.

Don't get me wrong: The Syrophoenician woman still has a lot to say to White congregations. She simultaneously challenges Jesus and humanizes those who might be "other." Her experience as a parent makes her immediately relatable and human to every parent who has held a sick child, but I should never preach her story without naming the realities of her situation. She is the "other," whom we would assume is different from us but whose humanity screams across millennia. I am coming to accept that I am way more like Matthew the tax collector than Peter the fisherman, more like Nicodemus the Pharisee than John the Baptist, more like Jairus than the Syrophoenician woman who shapes Jesus's future ministry.

For those of us who are waking up to the dynamics of privilege, racism, and heteronormativity in our church and society, we should increasingly shape the story of our lives with the stories of Acts. Paul's story offers deep lessons about how privilege can be leveraged for good—when to flex it, when to downplay it, and when to simply sit back and be quiet so that others can lead. He doesn't always get it right. Biblical narratives are sometimes cautionary tales. Story outcomes can offer big, glaring hints that sometimes a biblical character royally messed up. In Paul's imperfection are critical lessons for those of us who will try but sometimes get it wrong and then give it another go. I can see myself in that story, and I hope other White church leaders will too.

Why I Think White Church Leaders Should Pay More Attention to Paul

Aleze Fulbright

Although Paul is heralded as a foundational figure of the Christian faith for his contributions to the Christian movement, we cannot dismiss his beginnings or the ways he used his privilege as part of the deadly campaign to eliminate a segment of people for what they believed. Oftentimes, the church fails to remember the process of transformation and only holds up the transformed person. Dissecting the brutal beginnings of Paul's rise to power offers us an important lens through which we can see that, indeed, "grace is sufficient" (2 Corinthians 12:9, NRSVue). We can also see how our shameful past practices can be held in tension with Paul's own past, so that we can become a catalyst for long-term, sustainable change.

What's the Point of This Book?

Mike Baughman

We would all pay alarmed attention if literally any member of our congregation were to stand up and say, "I'm a part of this congregation, but because of the way I'm treated, I worry that my life doesn't matter." Because empathy is a core value of those who follow Christ, we would ask questions. We might get defensive at first, but we all know a healthy response would be to get over our defensiveness, recognize that this person is the greatest scholar of their own experience, and seek to understand what led them to experience hurt. At the very least, we'd do things to make them feel more valued, and at our best, we would actually value them more.

I'm consistently flummoxed by the White church's widespread failure to adequately address the Black Lives Matter movement. I've witnessed far more ecclesial apathy than empathy, more aggression than compassion, and more intentional ignorance than thoughtful concern. While clapping back "All lives matter" is the pastoral-care equivalent of telling a terminally ill person, "Everyone dies anyway, so get over it," it may still be better than the gobsmacking silence of those who claim to love Black people or gay people or immigrant people but are completely unwilling to sacrifice or even risk speaking out in support of the people they claim to love. Moments like now call for empathy, but we dare not stop there. We are living through a time in history that demands action that future generations will judge. One of my favorite church members used to say, "I'm just not interested in being a part of a congregation that's more worried about upsetting the applecart than they are about upsetting God."

One of my favorite bits of Scripture comes from Acts 17:6. Paul and Silas have been performing miracles, growing the church, healing people, and doing it all in nontraditional ways. While doing good, they've upset a lot of economic, cultural, and religious applecarts. A mob forms to take them down and complains to the authorities, "These people who have been turning the world upside down have come here also" (Acts 17:6, NRSVue). There are applecarts in our church and society that need to be upset if we are going to build the kind of kingdom for which God longs. This book is an effort to learn from Paul so that we might once again turn the world upside down to restore its proper order.

Why Exploring Paul and Privilege Is About Way More Than Just Black and White

Aleze Fulbright

In a period of heightened awareness, churches began adopting the language of "diversity and inclusion" and sought to remove offensive language from the lexicon. Yet far more intolerances—in language and otherwise—remain. Oftentimes, we dismiss these issues in the church. We mask our abdication of holding others accountable for their actions as Christ-love.

The church has been the greatest propagator of segregation and shameful acts against persons who are marginalized. The church that preaches about liberating those who are oppressed has become the oppressor through our toxic charity and our complicity to remain silent instead of speaking up for the very things that Jesus talks about throughout the Gospels. And I would suggest that even in our advocacy, we are highly selective about whom we advocate for, often leaving the most vulnerable to fend for themselves. To explore Paul and privilege is to hold up a mirror, dispel myths, and create commitments toward fulfilling the Micah 6:8 mandate "to do justice and to love kindness and to walk humbly with your God" (NRSVue). This book helps us learn from Paul so we might turn the world upside down to restore its proper order.

Reflection Questions

1. Are you nervous at all to read this book? What worries you about the potential content or how it might challenge you?

2. How do you feel about Mike's assertion that maybe he has put himself in too many stories from the gospel?

3. In what ways has the church advanced segregation and shameful acts against persons who are marginalized? In what ways has the church been a force for good in cultivating equity?

4. Why did you choose to read this book? What excites you about reading a book like this?

5. Mike realizes he is "way more like Matthew the tax collector than Peter the fisherman, more like Nicodemus the Pharisee than John the Baptist." Are there characters in the Gospels with whom you most identify? Why? Has that changed over time?

CHAPTER 1

Saul's Privilege

Power, Perspective, and the Peril of Unexamined Advantage (Acts 7; 22)

Aleze Fulbright

Introduction

Privilege is not a modern invention, though the illuminated messaging we use to describe it makes it appear as if it is a twenty-first-century occurrence. Long before sociologists named it, and centuries before theologians debated it, privilege functioned as an invisible architecture shaping access, authority, and voice. Privilege determined who was believed, who was protected, who could move freely, and whose suffering was rendered invisible. When read carefully, the biblical witness, especially the story of Saul of Tarsus, reveals how profoundly privilege can shape religious imagination, institutional loyalty, and even violence done in God's name.

As one who has been kissed by God's sun, reading Acts 7 and 22, I cannot approach Saul/Paul as a neutral character. My hermeneutical posture is informed by the lived experience of being both deeply committed to the church and historically marginalized by it, of loving Scripture while knowing it has been (and continues to be) weaponized, of honoring Paul's theological contributions while interrogating the systems that formed him.

This chapter does not seek to cancel Saul/Paul or to canonize him uncritically. Rather, I hope it offers a primer on privilege through Saul/Paul's story, attending to how his education, citizenship, gender, religious internship, and social standing shaped both his early persecution of the church and his later apostolic ministry—for better and for worse. By illuminating Saul's privilege, we are invited to see how similar dynamics operate in our own time.

Saul at the Feet of Power

Acts 7 introduces Saul not as a theologian or apostle but as a silent beneficiary of violence. Stephen, a Hellenistic Jewish believer, stands accused before the Sanhedrin. His sermon is brilliant, prophetic, and deeply unsettling. When the crowd turns on Stephen, they stone him. Luke makes a pointed note: "The witnesses laid their coats at the feet of a young man named Saul" (Acts 7:58, NRSVue).

This detail is not incidental. To hold the cloaks was to be a guardian of legitimacy. Saul is positioned as a trusted overseer, one whose presence authorizes the act. He is not throwing stones, but he is complicit. His privilege affords him proximity to power without exposure to consequences. We have seen this pattern throughout history, where privilege operates in this way, not always through direct action but through sanctioned silence.

I have seen, both from my corporate experience and in this sacred calling, how many times nonclergy persons allow the pastor to be undermined without defending them, knowing the truth they hold would make all the difference. I have seen times when my own integrity was questioned by people in positions of power and authority, and no one publicly rendered aid, and I, too, like Stephen, was silenced at the feet of those in power.

Education as Privilege

In Acts 22, Paul recounts his credentials before a hostile crowd: "I am a Jew born in Tarsus in Cilicia but brought up in this city at the feet of Gamaliel" (Acts 22:3, NRSVue). Gamaliel was among the most respected rabbis of the first century, associated with the school of Hillel. To be educated under him signaled elite theological formation, interpretive authority, and insider access.

As we know, education is never neutral. When I think about growing up in Tulsa, Oklahoma, I remember my elementary school, located in the heart of an underserved, historically excluded community. The books were dated, we had classrooms in prefabs, and the school ranked poorly on standardized tests. In middle school, I was among the few from my elementary school admitted to a magnet program. The difference was extreme, and I had a steep learning curve in my first year, struggling severely with the demands of the new school and the expectations placed on me without consideration of my background. I witnessed firsthand that those who were privileged to attend better elementary schools had a significant advantage and excelled in that learning environment.

Saul's training shaped not only what he knew but also how he understood faithfulness. His zeal was not ignorance; it was disciplined, credentialed, and affirmed. Willie James Jennings notes, "Theological education can either form people toward love or toward domination, depending on the social imagination it reinforces."[1] Paul's education empowered his ministry, but it also armed him with the tools to persecute others in God's name.

Roman Citizenship

Perhaps the most striking marker of Saul's privilege is his Roman citizenship. In Acts 22:25-29, when Saul/Paul is about to be flogged, he calmly asks, "Is it legal for you to flog a Roman person who is uncondemned?" (Acts 22:25, NRSVue). The proceedings stopped immediately. Fear replaces force. This moment reveals how the law functions differently depending on one's status. Roman citizenship conferred legal rights, enabled mobility, and provided protection from severe punishment. Paul carries his citizenship like a shield, sometimes invoking it strategically, other times holding it in reserve.

I cannot read this without thinking of the uneven application of law in the Americas. Citizenship on paper has never guaranteed embodied safety for Black bodies. From Dred Scott to Jim Crow to mass incarceration, legal status has not functioned as protection but often as a pretense.[2] Additionally, the ongoing debates and "othering" of those who desired to have the same freedoms and experiences continue to repeat themselves.

Yes, Paul's citizenship advanced the gospel. Paul's citizenship allowed him to appeal to Caesar and move freely across the empire. Yet it also insulated him from the kind of bodily vulnerability experienced by enslaved persons, women, and the poor. Paul's theology of suffering must be read alongside the protections he possessed.

Gender and Patriarchy

Saul's maleness is so assumed in the text that it is rarely named. In the first-century Roman society, being male conferred authority, mobility, and credibility. Saul travels freely, addresses assemblies, receives formal training, and exercises public power—opportunities categorically denied to most women of that time. While Paul later affirms women as coworkers—including Phoebe, Priscilla, and Junia—his letters also reflect patriarchal assumptions that have been used to silence women across centuries.[3]

I, as a Black woman, read Paul's story alongside those of Hagar, Mary, and the unnamed women whose labor sustained movements they did not control, while understanding and knowing that without the women, the witness could not be expanded. While they were silenced or not provided opportunities for a platform, they were instrumental in the good news being shared broadly, despite the limitations placed on them simply because of their gender and the patriarchal structures.

Conversion Does Not Erase Formation

Paul's legacy challenges us to ask, *How often do we benefit from systems we critique but do not dismantle?* Privilege does not disappear when one is converted; it must be continually examined.

Paul describes himself as "zealous for God" (Acts 22:3, NRSVue), operating with letters of authorization from the high priest (Acts 9:1-2). This is not rogue fanaticism; it is institutionally sanctioned violence. Saul is, in effect, an intern of the religious establishment. Internship is privilege when it provides access, mentorship, and institutional trust. Saul's authority to arrest believers emerges from his proximity to power. Paul does not question the system because the system affirms him. He was formed by this understanding, which he carried with him throughout his life. This formation guided him to believe he was doing what was right in the name of the system.

We further recognize Paul's privilege in Acts 9, which recounts Saul's dramatic conversion. Yet Acts 22 reminds us that his story is not erased but reinterpreted. Paul never denies his past; he reframes it. Paul's privilege remains, but its purpose is transformed. However, the transformation is imbalanced. Paul's letters reflect both radical inclusion and lingering hierarchy. Paul proclaims freedom in Christ while negotiating household codes. He advocates unity while centering his own authority.

This tension mirrors the American church's post–civil rights era and even modern practices—formal integration without full equity, inclusive language without redistributed power. Privilege, when unexamined, reproduces itself even in redeemed communities.

Conclusion

The question is not whether Paul had privilege. The question is whether the church today will acknowledge its own. Paul's privilege allowed him to shape Christian theology profoundly. This is a gift. However, it also requires us to be cautious not to confuse access with righteousness in Paul's formation. Privilege can amplify the gospel or distort it.

Saul's story is not a condemnation of privilege but a call to accountability. Privilege is power, and power demands ethical scrutiny. I believe that when surrendered to Christ, privilege can be leveraged for liberation. However, when left unexamined, it becomes a tool for harm.

The gospel does not require us to divest ourselves of identity, but it does require us to tell the truth about it.

Learning at the feet of Gamaliel, the cloak at Stephen's death, and the shield of Roman citizenship shaped Paul. And if we are honest, they shape us still. It is through the humility of naming them that we can hope to be transformed beyond them.

Reflection Questions

1. Saul was educated "at the feet of Gamaliel." This is a unique and rare education. What benefits do you suspect this may have served him later in life as he became a co-conspirator with the oppressed? How might an exclusive education opportunity make it more difficult for him to advocate for justice?

2. One could easily view a young Saul and assume that because he had access to power, he was also righteous. When is proximity to power sometimes mistaken for spiritual maturity or spiritual wisdom? Can proximity to power increase spiritual maturity or wisdom?

3. Saul held the cloaks at Stephen's stoning—not throwing stones himself, but complicit through sanctioned silence. Where in your life or church have you "held the cloaks," not actively causing harm but remaining silent because the issue did not impact you?

4. Could Saul have saved Stephen? Why or why not?

5. Aleze offers, "Privilege is power, and power demands ethical scrutiny." Whether it is because of a title at work, a role in the family, or a place in society, so many people legitimately fail to see how much power they have. How can people get better at seeing the extent of power and influence they have? What specific practices or relationships in your life help you see your influence and maintain ethical scrutiny? Who has permission to call you out?

"I Live and Die a Member of the Church of England"

Ashley Boggan

Any honest account of John Wesley must begin not with his marginality but with his privilege. Wesley was not an outsider to power. He was formed by it, educated within it, and authorized by it. To understand how Methodism emerged—and why Wesley fought so fiercely to keep it *within* the Church of England—we must reckon with how deliberately he used the advantages afforded to him by birth, education, race, gender, and ecclesial status.

Wesley was a White English male in the eighteenth century, born into a clerical household at Epworth Rectory. As the son of Samuel Wesley, an ordained priest, John inherited not only theological formation but also cultural legitimacy. He was educated at Charterhouse School and then at the University of Oxford, one of the most elite institutions in England. Oxford did not merely confer intellectual training; it marked Wesley as a gentleman, a person whose voice carried weight in church and society. His ordination as a priest in the Church of England further embedded him within the intertwined structures of church and state. To be an Anglican priest in the eighteenth century was to be an agent of both religious authority and civic order.[4]

Wesley knew this. He did not romanticize his position, nor did he pretend that Methodism was born from the margins. Instead, he intentionally built a reform movement *inside* the Church of England, precisely because remaining within it preserved the privileges that protected both him and his followers. As long as Methodists were Anglicans, they could preach, organize societies, publish tracts, and travel the countryside with a degree of legal and social cover unavailable to dissenters. Separation would have meant loss of sacramental legitimacy, vulnerability to persecution, and exclusion from parish life.

This is why Wesley resisted schism with near-obsessive determination. He repeatedly insisted, "I live and die a member of the Church of England."[5] This was not mere sentimentality. It was strategic ecclesiology. Wesley understood that Methodism's ability to survive—and to press its critique of spiritual complacency—depended on staying within the institutional church, even when that church resisted him. His privilege as an ordained Anglican priest allowed him to defend Methodist preaching, discipline, and lay leadership against charges of enthusiasm or disorder. When magistrates or bishops objected, Wesley could speak as one of their own.

Crucially, Wesley did not use his privilege to shield himself alone. He leveraged it to defend Methodists—especially lay preachers—who had far less protection. He intervened with local authorities, wrote sharply worded letters to hostile clergy, and published reasoned defenses of Methodist practice. His status allowed him to insist that Methodist preaching was not rebellion but reform, not disorder but a return to scriptural Christianity. For Wesley, privilege became a tool for movement-building rather than self-preservation.

At the same time, Wesley used his authority to hold other ordained preachers accountable to the teachings of Jesus. He did not hesitate to name the spiritual failures of clergy who neglected the poor, avoided evangelism, or reduced Christianity to moral respectability. From his sermons and journals to his trenchant tracts, Wesley challenged fellow priests for preaching a gospel that demanded little and transformed less. His critique carried force precisely because he spoke as an insider—an Oxford-educated priest calling the church back to its own professed faith.

Nowhere is this clearer than in Wesley's insistence on social holiness. He used the credibility of his position to argue that justification by faith must lead to lives marked by mercy, discipline, and love of neighbor. He confronted clergy who dismissed the poor, ignored prisoners, or spiritualized away Jesus's commands. Wesley's privilege gave him access to pulpits, print, and platforms—and he spent that capital relentlessly on proclaiming a gospel that unsettled comfort and demanded accountability.

John Wesley's legacy, then, is not one of renouncing privilege but of *redeeming* it. He understood that privilege becomes spiritually dangerous when it is used to avoid risk or maintain complacency. Instead, Wesley treated his advantages as responsibilities. He stayed within the Church of England not to protect himself but to protect a movement aimed at renewing the church's faithfulness to Jesus Christ.

In Wesley's hands, privilege became a means of amplification: amplifying the gospel, amplifying the voices of the neglected, and amplifying the demand that the church live up to its calling. That disciplined, intentional use of power—rooted in accountability rather than entitlement—remains one of the most instructive aspects of his witness.

CHAPTER 2
The Call to Constant Conversion
(Acts 9)

Mike Baughman

Meeting Ananias

Every time I say the following sentence, I feel like the lamest human being on the planet: I learned about spoken word poetry from a TED talk. A few weeks later, while planning a date, I scanned the internet and discovered a spoken word event at a club I'd never heard of called Brooklyn's in South Dallas. I arrived about ten minutes before my date, and now begins the story that I'm really not proud of. Setting foot in Brooklyn's, I was immediately uncomfortable as a record scratch tore across my brain—I was the only White person in a very full club of Black people.

I wanted to leave.

My gut was to call my date and suggest we find something else to do, as deeply embarrassed as I would be to tell her why. As I turned toward the door, my friend Aleze popped into my brain. She steps into rooms and buildings full of White people all the time. How could I look her in the eyes if I walked out of this club? I started to turn back into Brooklyn's.

My White progressive perspective offered another crutch: *What if I'm intruding? What if I'm ruining a safe place?* Relieved to have an excuse for leaving that I could tell my date without hanging my head too low, I turned to leave.

"Excuse me," a raspy voice interrupted my retreat as a hand touched my elbow. I turned.

"Are you a poet?" A tall, muscular Black man with an on-brand poet goatee was looking me sincerely in the eye.

"What?" I mumbled, surprised that someone had broken the spell of an internal struggle I thought no one could see.

"Are you a poet? My name is Mike Guinn. I'm the emcee. I saw the iPad in your hand and thought you might be here to share some poetry. Don't want to leave anyone out."

To this day, those words cut me with love: "Don't want to leave anyone out."

After an awkward beat, I finally responded, "No, I'm not. Thanks. I'm just here to meet a friend, and I'm not sure if she's—"

"I'm pretty sure there are some seats over there if you want to wait for her. Glad you're here." He resumed recruiting poets as I made my way to an empty table. An imaginary spotlight followed me across a very crowded room full of people who I was convinced were looking at me—much more likely, they were looking at their poems or their dates or their phones. I texted my date, "I'm at Brooklyn's on the far side of the room. It shouldn't be too hard to find me."

She arrived fifteen minutes later after a very helpful hostess greeted her with, "I think your party might be over there," and pointed at my table.

The night was magic. I had adored Sarah Kay's TED talk poetry[1] on a computer screen, but I fell in love with spoken word that night over a beverage, a crackled microphone, and the collective celebration of a crowd who supported every poet on that stage. I've since performed original pieces, hosted spoken-word nights at a coffee shop/church, incorporated spoken-word poets into worship, and provided space for Mike Guinn to empower teen voices through spoken word.

The kindness of Mike Guinn, an Ananias in my life, changed me forever.

Conversion Stories (Acts 9:1-2)

True conversion always requires more than one encounter. My trip to Brooklyn's was one in a long line of experiences past and future that will help me make the movement from being a participant in oppressive systems to resisting oppressive forces. Saul's story is far more extreme than that of the average likely reader for this book. Saul was oppressive in his mindset (Acts 8:1) and in his actions (Acts 8:3; 9:1-2) and clearly contributed to a system that valued some lives (Jews who were complacent with Rome) over others (Christians). His conversion is extreme and sudden. I'm going to go out on a limb and assume that there aren't many card-carrying members of the KKK or Proud Boys reading this book. The average reader's "conversion experience" will not be nearly so dramatic as Saul's, nor will it be so sudden. White Americans have been largely untrained by society to talk about race—we haven't had to do so because Whiteness is the norm in much of society. A lifetime of subtle and overt white supremacy has influenced us. It may take a lifetime to dismantle it as well. Saul's conversion to Paul gives us a hyperbolic formula for understanding the kind of continual conversion we can and must seek if we are to accept the baptismal vow to "resist evil, injustice, and oppression in whatever forms they present themselves."[2]

Journeys to Damascus (Acts 9:3)

If you look at an ethnographic map of Dallas, Texas, you will see that people live in the city divided by race and think, "It's almost like it was designed that way." That's because redlining policies adopted by the Dallas city council at the turn of the twentieth century still shape the city today. If I had known Dallas better in 2011, I could have guessed that Brooklyn's would have a primarily Black customer base. At that time in my life, I considered myself to be against racism, but an honest inventory of where I lived and who I spent time with reveals that I rarely left my White suburban comfort zone of home and church. Just as Paul had to go to Damascus, a new place to him where the early church flourished, I needed to leave the White enclaves of North Dallas for a place where Black culture was thriving. Brooklyn's was one of my many Damascus journeys.

Instinctively, Christians know the value of breaking routine and comfort. One of the most consistently important experiences for religious growth is pilgrimage—a practice predicated on the notion that we can only find home by leaving it. We cannot learn and understand our own assumptions, culture, and values until we step out of them. This is especially true for anyone who is a part of the dominant culture within a society. It is difficult for many White Americans to identify their distinct culture and assumptions because it is such a part of the dominant culture. White churches typically assume that they are welcoming to everybody and don't recognize that the practices, habits, and culture that signal "welcome" to non-White Americans are frequently something very different from what their White churches offer.

One does not have to leave one's home to at least begin the journey of cultural pilgrimage. In a world where we are beginning to find authentic expressions of non-White culture through film, television, podcasts, books, and beyond, it is incumbent on White folks to start engaging with media that is written, directed, and created by non-White people. Movies like *The Farewell* offer a view into Chinese culture that pressed me to reconsider my understanding of death and family while also making me a better pastor to Asian American/Pacific Islander members of my congregation. *Hamilton* is right there on Disney+, raising questions of American identity through casting choices. *Watchmen* exposes audiences to history that far too few Americans know. The list goes on.

If you want your Damascus experiences, start by connecting with authentic expressions of non-White culture, but please do not stop there. There is something significant about literally moving your feet and driving your car to a new place. If you are White, put yourself in places where you are the only White person in a restaurant, community meeting, or church service. Leave your routine and see what God reveals.

Be Convicted, Accept Your Blind Spots, and Receive Help (Acts 9:4-5)

We cannot repent of a sin until we've named it. We cannot name a sin until we recognize it.

An important part of Saul's conversion is his conviction. Jesus calls out to Saul while a light from heaven encircles the traveling rabbi,

"Saul, Saul, why do you persecute me?" (Acts 9:4, NRSVue). When Saul asks who is calling him out, the heavenly voice replies, "I am Jesus, whom you are persecuting" (Acts 9:5, NRSVue). Making the transition from someone who is complicit in oppressive systems to someone who actively works against oppression will require some measure of feeling convicted. Because we White people are not trained to see our biases, they must be called out before they can be eliminated. Because heterosexuals aren't instinctively hurt by heteronormativity and men aren't instinctively hurt by patriarchy, those of us who fall into these categories need help seeing our blind spots. Our sins must be named. We must confess them. But no one likes to have their sins named.

On April 29, 2017, a police officer shot fifteen-year-old Jordan Edwards in the back of the head. The teen was riding in the passenger seat of a friend's car. They were peacefully leaving a party in Balch Springs, Texas, which is just a few miles from my house. Neither Edwards nor the car he was in posed a threat to the officer who fired. Two weeks later, charges had still not been filed against Oliver, the police officer who murdered Edwards.

I posted a link on Facebook to an article about the case with the following text: "This is a nightmare. Decency demands homicide charges are brought against Oliver. We're not even talking about justice . . . basic decency demands it. I thought Dallas was better than this." To which Michelle Williams, a Dallas leader whom I deeply respect, commented: "Why? Why did you think Dallas was better than this, friend? You are surrounded by men and women of color who have been screaming this at the top of our lungs for years!"

I saw her post and immediately felt defensive. The following thoughts raced through my brain. I am not proud of them: *Doesn't she see I'm an ally? Doesn't she know how hard I work for justice? Why can't she see my best intentions? You know what, I'm just not going to post or even talk about race anymore!*

By some miracle of the Holy Spirit, I did not fire off a defensive response. I stopped and thought about her words. Eventually, I recognized the gift she offered. She could have written me off. She could have unfriended me. I had hurt her. Still, she called me "friend." She thought I would know better. It hurts when the people you think are friends don't see how painful your realities are—how day-to-day inequities burden your soul. I did that to her. I failed to see her.

It is important for those of us with privilege to hear critique, see it as the gift that it is, and then repent of our sin by changing our perspective and behavior. In our effort to help, we will get it wrong. In our desire to heal, we will occasionally hurt. Choosing to no longer engage is a choice to retreat into privilege and away from our calling to "resist evil, injustice, and oppression in whatever forms they present themselves."[3] *Because oppressive systems are such a part of our world, we, like Saul on the ground, will be disoriented by what we see and hear, but we absolutely must be disoriented by what we cannot see as well.* Many of us with privilege are blind to the experiences of others, even when we believe our vision to be 20/20. Disorientation is necessary for growth. Opening ourselves to receive critique is one of the critical steps to becoming a co-conspirator with those who have been marginalized.

Travel in Community and Follow God's Guidance (Acts 9:6-8)

Saul does not stand up on his own. His travel companions pick him up off the ground and point him in the right direction. Do not miss the fact that Saul made the choice to follow Jesus's command. He could have stumbled his way back to Jerusalem for Pharisee reinforcements. Instead, he heard God's voice, accepted direction, and walked in community. Generally speaking, society does not teach privileged people how to dismantle systems of oppression. It is difficult work. We cannot do this work alone.

I love leading pilgrimages, including ones to sites important to the American Civil Rights Movement. On one such pilgrimage, I took a group of high school students to Selma, Alabama. After walking across the Edmund Pettus Bridge and hearing stories about the march to Birmingham, we spent time with a seasoned saint who was fourteen years old when she marched halfway across the bridge on Bloody Sunday. She shared her daily routine for the weeks leading up to the 1965 march for voters' rights. People would meet for worship, hear their directions for the day, and then perform whatever action organizers had planned. One of my youth group members asked, "Why did you waste time worshipping God every morning?"

It wasn't my proudest moment as a youth pastor.

"Excuse me?" our host asked. She was a bit stunned by the question.

"Why did you waste time worshipping God every morning instead of just meeting up and then going to the protest or whatever?" the teen elaborated.

The civil rights leader smiled. "Because it's hard work changing the world, young lady, and we needed to be reminded—every single day—that we were connected to a power greater than ourselves."

Worship was a means not only to connect with God's power and hear God's calling but also to learn from one another how to go about the hard work of fighting for justice. They learned patience from one another and built strength as a community. They learned how to pick one another up and remain on the path before them. We, too, must do this work together. We cannot work for equity alone; we need the power of community and the presence of God to change ourselves enough so that we can change the world.

Go to Damascus and Spend Time with Ananias (Acts 9:10-19)

To move from oppressor to co-conspirator with the oppressed, we must not only go to "Damascus"; we must also meet the people there and find God in them. Damascus was, for Saul, a place where Christianity had taken hold with strength and little fear of persecution. Saul had less power in Damascus. I've found Damascus in Brooklyn's nightclub. I've found Damascus while worshipping at Birmingham's 16th Street Baptist Church. I've found Damascus in Round Up and Alexandre's, two of Dallas's most famous gay bars. I've found Damascus in the performing arts community, where churchy actors are rare for good reason. Most important, I've seen God at work in the people who live, play, work, and find comfort in those places that feel like Damascus to those with privilege.

There are plenty of Ananiases out there to teach us. I need to offer some caution, though. I can imagine a lot of well-intentioned folks would come to this section and appoint their Asian American friend to be their Ananias and miss that doing so asks that person to take on significant risk and emotional labor. God's call upon Ananias to shepherd Saul put Ananias's life in jeopardy. People who have been marginalized by society similarly risk a great deal when they approach people in power and challenge their assumptions about systems of oppression—even when the person in power asks them to do so. When a woman pastor chooses not to challenge the patriarchal assumption of her bishop, it isn't because she thinks the bishop does a great job holding space for women to thrive; it might mean that it just wasn't worth the risk. There is an art to holding brave space with someone when it starts with your own vulnerability. Note that Saul's privilege and power are largely removed before God asks Ananias to care for Saul. First demonstrate your willingness to let go of power and privilege and then see whether an Ananias welcomes you in.

It will help to start by exploring YouTube, print media, blogs, and books that share BIPOC (Black, Indigenous, and people of color) experiences, discuss queer theology, and amplify female narratives. Read Amanda Gorman, Cole Arthur Riley, Langston Hughes, or Audre Lorde and let their poetry break your soul. Many with marginalized voices have shared their emotional labor with the world. Lean on them. Hear God in them. Saul sought out Ananias *and believed Jesus spoke through him.* Engage people authentically. Ask informed questions with vulnerability and humility. Do this work, and you will likely discover Ananiases all around you who will invite you into their worlds. Remember, in those spaces, you are a guest who has much to learn and nothing to correct.

Suffer and Be Humble (Acts 9:16, 23-25)

Saul/Paul suffered for the sake of the gospel, and so shall we. Jesus doesn't promise a lollipop. He promises a cross. In our pursuit of equity, those of us who have "more" must, from time to time, hold on to less—less talking time, less decision-making authority, and less wealth. Equity is not free, but it does lead to more freedom for everyone. There is an art to leveraging privilege for equity and stepping back so that others can speak. Those who wish to work for equity will suffer as must all who seek to realize God's kingdom on earth. The work that lies ahead is not easy, but it is good. We lose our lives so that we might gain abundant life (Matthew 16:25; John 10:10).

Building Credibility and Allies (Acts 9:20-28)

Until I began working on this project, I always missed an element of Saul's story that is totally predictable—that Christians were terrified of him. After years of actively persecuting them, Paul struggled to gain credibility with the people he was trying to help. I sometimes assume that others can see and trust my intentions. I forget that even if I haven't actively hurt the person across a table from me, that person may have been hurt by one hundred people who look or act like me. I can never step into a pastoral care situation with a gay man or a collegial relationship with a Black woman and assume that they will give me the benefit of the doubt.

When Black folks give White folks the side-eye and when queer persons are reticent to trust church leaders, it is not because they are racist or discriminatory against White people or our religion. They have had to learn survival techniques to endure the very real harm done by oppressive systems in their lives. It was church people who threw rocks at Matthew Shepard's head. It was church people who enslaved Africans. It was church people who performed genocide against the people native to the Americas.

Aleze once advised me, "You have got to be consistent in your conversion [from oppressor to co-conspirator] so that you have the allies you need." We tend to think that White people are allies to Black people and clergy are allies to gay people, but not the opposite. While I am sometimes an ally to Aleze, she is an ally for me in places where I do not fit in, including places of church authority that have nothing to do with the color of her skin and everything to do with the fact that I'm all kinds of awkward around bishops. Mike Guinn is my Ananias in spoken-word worlds, where I sometimes babble in the face of eloquence.

After years, friends like Aleze, Michelle, and Mike trust and vouch for me or, at least, my intentions. They do not expect perfection from me—thank God! They will stand by me because they trust that I will learn from my missteps and that something in me is worth investing in. For that, I am deeply grateful. They will sometimes ask me to take a hit, to take a risk, and to do so for equity's sake. LGBTQ+-identifying members of my congregation have asked a lot of me, but none of it comes close to what they risk just by being openly gay in Texas. On my better days, I am eager to sacrifice for them. On my less-than-better days, I do it anyway. On my worst days, I retreat into my privilege and make up some excuse. Jesus doesn't promise a lollipop. He promises a cross. We church folk who care about equity have to know there will be a price.

Reflection Questions

1. What road to Damascus experiences have pushed you beyond your places of comfort? What did you learn about yourself and privilege in those spaces? Where might God be calling you to have more Damascus road experiences?

2. When has your privilege been named by someone else? How did you react? What did you learn?

3. Who are some Ananiases who have played a role in allowing the "scales [to fall] from [your] eyes" (Acts 9:18, NRSVue)?

4. What price might you have to pay to bring about equity? Are you willing to sacrifice for it?

Conversion to Freedom

Ashley Boggan

Isabella Baumfree was born into a world where her name, her body, and even her future were treated as property. Around 1797, in Ulster County, New York, she entered life enslaved, speaking Dutch before she ever learned English, raised under the harsh instability of being bought and sold. As a young woman, she endured the violence and grief that slavery demanded: family separations, exhausting labor, and the constant knowledge that injustice could reach into every corner of ordinary life. Yet even in those years, Isabella carried a spiritual hunger—an awareness that the God she heard whispered about must surely see more than the enslavers claimed.[4]

In the early decades of the nineteenth century, Isabella's life was marked not only by suffering but also by a growing interior strength. New York was moving slowly toward emancipation, but freedom came unevenly, and Isabella's experience of bondage remained brutal. She married an enslaved man, Thomas, and bore children, only to watch slavery threaten the bonds of motherhood. When she eventually walked away from her enslaver in 1826, carrying her infant daughter with her, she stepped into freedom with trembling courage. That physical journey was also a spiritual one: a movement from captivity toward the possibility of God's promise.

But Isabella's deepest transformation was not merely legal. It was inward. She later testified that in her darkest hours, she cried out to God with an intensity that was raw and unpolished. Her prayers were not the refined petitions of the privileged; they were the desperate pleadings of someone who had nowhere else to turn. In those cries, Isabella came to believe she encountered the living Christ—not as an abstract doctrine but as a present Savior who heard the oppressed.

Her conversion experience unfolded as an awakening and a calling. She spoke of coming to know Jesus as the one who could break chains stronger than iron: chains of fear, despair, and dehumanization. The God of Scripture became, for her, the God who had walked with Israel out of Egypt, the God who had not abandoned the enslaved. She was converted not to private comfort but to holy purpose.

In 1843, Isabella took a step as radical as any road walked by the apostles: She left behind her birth name and became Sojourner Truth. "Sojourner," because she understood herself as a traveler sent by God. "Truth," because she believed the gospel demanded honesty about the world as it was—and courage to proclaim what it should be. Like Saul of Tarsus, struck blind on the road to Damascus, Isabella experienced a renaming that marked a new identity. Saul, once a persecutor, rose as Paul, apostle to the Gentiles. Isabella, once enslaved, rose as Sojourner Truth, preacher to the nation.

Paul's conversion was not simply a change of mind; it was a turning of direction. The one who had upheld oppression through violence became the one who suffered for the sake of

Christ. Sojourner's conversion was similarly disruptive. The woman who had been told she was less than human became a witness to divine justice. Her faith did not allow her to accept the world's false order. Conversion made her dangerous to injustice.

Sojourner began traveling, preaching, singing, and testifying in camp meetings, abolitionist gatherings, and women's rights conventions. She spoke with a prophetic force that came from experience and conviction: God had delivered her, and therefore she could not be silent while others remained bound. Her famous question—"Ain't I a woman?"—was not merely rhetoric.[5] It was theology. It was a declaration that the image of God cannot be owned, diminished, or denied.

Like Paul, she carried the gospel into public life. Paul crossed boundaries of Jew and Gentile, slave and free. Sojourner crossed boundaries of race, gender, and class, insisting that Christ's salvation was inseparable from justice. Conversion, for both, was not an escape from the world but a commissioning into it.

Isabella Baumfree became Sojourner Truth because Christ met her on her road—out of slavery, into freedom, and onward into prophetic witness. Her life proclaims the same gospel Paul learned in Damascus: When Jesus calls a person by name, they do not remain what the world has made them. They become what God intends—messengers of liberation, truth, and transforming grace.

CHAPTER 3
Genital Conference
(Acts 15; 16:11-15)

Mike Baughman

Institutional Correction

When a marginalized community builds an institution to protect the shared lessons and experiences that bind it together, that newly formed institution sometimes commits the same sins of marginalization as it figures out its new identity. The early church struggled with this, at times welcoming Gentiles into the community but not trusting them as leaders unless they were circumcised. At other times, the early church outright rejected Gentiles who would not accept circumcision. The Jerusalem Council (Acts 15) is an example of those with institutional privilege dismantling harm through direct advocacy, institutional cover, and embodied solidarity. Well-established institutions that may or may not have (but definitely have) done harm ought to pay attention. To learn from their example, first we need to talk a bit about circumcision.

Circumcision: It Used to Be Kind of a Big Deal

Any time circumcision comes up in a Bible study with teenagers, one brave student will raise their hand to ask the question that half the room is wondering: "What is circumcision?" Answering the question results in wide eyes, strings of comments full of double entendre, more than a few laughs, and at least one student asking why on earth God would demand such a thing. Mention circumcision in a sermon, and about even numbers of adult congregants will either shift uncomfortably, make a joke to their neighbor, or look very academic and serious. Apart from our general American discomfort discussing genitalia in church, circumcision feels to most like a "nothing issue." Congregants find it strange, silly, or even primitive that some people in the Bible care about foreskin status.

It is easy to forget that circumcision was one of the most settled and established practices for those who worshipped the God of Israel. First-century Jews did not question its importance, legitimacy, or necessity. The Bible consistently repeats the requirement in no uncertain terms. From the moment Abraham said to God, "You want me to do what now?" (see Genesis 17:10) to the time of the early disciples, circumcision was an important ritual for those who worshipped the God of Israel. It offered a clear, definitive marker to identify which men were in the covenant and which men were not. If sacraments are defined as "outward, visible signs of an inward spiritual grace," circumcision was nearly sacramental.[1] This wasn't just an external marker in ancient gym locker rooms and community baths. Urination, sex, and bathing served as regular, ongoing reminders to Jewish men that they share in a covenant with God—a covenant that called them to sacrifice and make different choices than the rest of society. Circumcision set them apart. Circumcision is a tool for discipleship. Circumcision was sacred.

Perhaps because Jesus commanded the disciples to make disciples of all nations (Matthew 28:19) by baptizing them but not requiring circumcision, general practice allowed Gentiles to join the church without genital modification. They were not, however, allowed to lead. The practice of viewing some as second-class citizens reared its head again and again throughout the history of the church and continues today. In my own Methodist tradition, we see this same pattern with marginalized people who were allowed to participate but not fully lead:

- John Wesley licensed women to preach, and The United Brethren Church made Lydia Sexton a pulpit speaker, but neither considered women suitable for ordination because of their gender.
- Harry Hoosier, a Black man, preached in the 1784 Christmas Conference that formed The Methodist Episcopal Church but was denied voice and vote in formal proceedings—his gifts were welcome; his authority was not.
- The Methodist Episcopal Church ordained Richard Allen, a Black man, but relegated his worship participation to the balcony in any established White church. They left him out, so he left to form Mother Bethel and the AME Church, which still ministers apart from The United Methodist Church today.
- Through most of the twentieth century, Black men could serve as bishops but only to supervise Black clergy.
- Women could raise money and do the work of the church but could not lead as clergy until 1886 in The Methodist Protestant Church, 1889 in The United Brethren Church, and 1956 in The Methodist Church.

- From 1968 to 2024, self-affirming openly gay persons joined United Methodist churches but could not lead them or be married in them.
- Although women make up the majority of United Methodist clergy in the United States, fewer than a handful of women serve as senior pastors of the one hundred largest United Methodist churches.

Second-class citizenship in the kingdom of God persists even when it is no longer overt, and marginalized communities have been consistently told, "Join but don't lead. Participate but know your place."

To frame how radical the Jerusalem Council may be (see Acts 15), the biblical case for circumcision is far stronger than any condemnation of female clergy, same-gender sex, fluid gender identities, or the razor-thin scriptural justifications misused to support white supremacy. It is in this context that "some people came down from Judea teaching the family of believers, 'Unless you are circumcised according to the custom we've received from Moses, you can't be saved'" (Acts 15:1). They had sound biblical arguments, but "teaching the *family* of believers" (emphasis added) suggests a broad-based campaign to ensure certain people held second-class citizenship in the kingdom of God. The Jerusalem Council poses key questions to the contemporary church:

- Is it more faithful to the Scriptures to attend strictly to a literalist interpretation or to embody the kind of radical openness expressed by the Jerusalem Council?
- How can those privileged with institutional authority and respect follow the witness of the Jerusalem Council to turn our current systems upside down?

Privileged Co-conspirators: Risk Your Credibility and Commit

While not revered like the original disciples of Jesus, Paul and Barnabas established their credibility within the early church. As men privileged with institutional acceptance, they do several noteworthy things in Acts 15 and 16:11-15. First, they dedicate themselves to specializing in ministry with Gentiles. Cross-cultural ministry is difficult and risky. Church leaders who have not served in cross-cultural contexts view pastors who do so successfully as oddities or as people who instinctively connect with people, something that eludes most pastors. In so doing, they diminish the hard work, study, self-examination, risk, and commitment it takes to engage across cultures. Institutionally accepted leaders take a huge risk when they turn leadership over to those the institution devalues. It's a gamble. If the gamble does not pay off, Paul and Barnabas would have surely lost credibility and respect with many people lining up to say, "We told them it was a crazy idea." First and foremost, Paul and Barnabas *invest in people unlike them.*

When I launched a new church that would specifically build ministry with emerging generations and queer Dallasites who had been burned by the church, I had a lot of detractors. I am embarrassed by how much time I spent trying to convince others that what we were trying was a good idea—even after we had funding and the required level of support from our denomination! I kept campaigning. I don't know whether I was motivated primarily by a desire to build support for the movement or to protect myself if everything fell apart.

Convincing detractors distracted me from our mission. A well-established layperson and wise friend called me on the phone and advised me, "Stop trying to convince everyone. They've already made up their minds that you're crazy. Just put your head down, make this church work, and they won't have a dang thing to say." It was some of the best advice I received when church planting. Paul and Barnabas could not have "traveled through Phoenicia and Samaria, telling stories about the conversion of the Gentiles to everyone" (Acts 15:3) if they had spent all of their time trying to convince apostles in Jerusalem that this ministry was a good idea. Because they ministered with the Gentiles, they could report fruits of the Spirit and evidence of God's work that "thrilled the brothers and sisters" (Acts 15:3) in Jerusalem and beyond.

Imagine what Gentile converts felt when established Christians mounted campaigns to undermine their membership or leadership in the church. Gentile leaders had been taught about the God of Israel, Jesus, and the Holy Spirit. They'd heard stories of Jesus's ministry with the Syrophoenician woman and Gentiles who lived on the far banks of the Sea of Galilee. The Gentile leaders in Antioch, Syria, and Cilicia gave their lives, passion, expertise, money, and time to the church only to hear other Jesus followers tell them they did not belong. The "people [who] came down from Judea" (Acts 15:1) were not only undermining Paul and Barnabas's successes in ministry; they were actively harming the emotional and spiritual well-being of people Paul and Barnabas loved. Acts 15:2 perhaps undersells the degree to which Paul and Barnabas "argued strongly against" those who opposed Gentile conversion without circumcision. In Paul's Letter to the Galatians, who were being harassed about circumcision, he says rather bluntly, "I wish that the ones who are upsetting you would castrate themselves!" (Galatians 5:12). Paul and Barnabas *get mad on behalf of the people with whom they are in ministry and take a public stance in support of their ministry co-laborers who have been marginalized.* We don't have letters from Gentile leaders. Luke doesn't record their pain, but reading between the lines of Paul's fury, we can sense their anguish and feel Paul's solidarity.

It matters when marginalized communities *see* people with privilege fighting on behalf of those who are marginalized! It builds trust. One of my mentors in this regard would tell people how long it took her to trust that White folks would advocate for her even when she wasn't in the room. She almost needs to see privileged leaders fighting for her when they do not know she's watching—not because she thinks White people are bad but because systems reward conformity so much so that many White people say all the nice, inclusive things to colleagues of color or from public podiums but buckle under the pressure of institutional patterns of oppression when real decisions are on the line. When White colleagues prove themselves over time—taking hits and risks, demonstrating consistent commitment—that's when she trusts that they might just be co-conspirators. Contemporary leaders should take note of Paul and Barnabas's consistent advocacy for the people with whom they ministered. Paul knew their pain well enough to craft the Letter to the Galatians. They risked their career, calling, and credibility. It is not enough to only advocate when it is safe to do so.

Institutional Cover

Not everyone is called to be in direct ministry with those who have been oppressed or marginalized. Most of the apostles continued to be in ministry with circumcised Jews and never followed in Paul's footsteps. Still, without Peter and James, Barnabas and Paul would not likely have won the day at the Jerusalem Council. While more proven and institutionally accepted than Gentile leaders in Antioch and Galatia, Paul and Barnabas didn't have near the institutional authority the original disciples enjoyed. Regardless of how steeped they are in privilege, every innovative church planter who ministers with those not in the mainstream of the church needs allies who lend institutional cover. My ministry as a straight, ordained pastor with queer communities only survived denominational approval because of the support offered by people who built their church leadership credibility through very traditional means. Decision makers heard their voices differently than they heard mine. Peter flexes his authority before defending the Gentiles alongside Paul and Barnabas's ministry:

> *"Fellow believers, you know that, early on, God chose me from among you as the one through whom the Gentiles would hear the word of the gospel and come to believe. God, who knows people's deepest thoughts and desires, confirmed this by giving them the Holy Spirit, just as he did to us. He made no distinction between us and them, but purified their deepest thoughts and desires through faith. Why then are you now challenging God by placing a burden on the shoulders of these disciples that neither we nor our ancestors could bear? On the contrary, we believe that we and they are saved in the same way, by the grace of the Lord Jesus."*
>
> *(Acts 15:7b-11)*

After Peter offered his support, "the entire assembly fell quiet as they listened to Barnabas and Paul describe all the signs and wonders God did among the Gentiles through their activity" (Acts 15:12).

One of the "Peter"s who defended my ministry with folks on the LGBTQ+ spectrum, who required ministry in new ways, used to tell the story of an old family axe. "This axe," he'd say while showing a picture, "is the same axe that my great-grandfather used when he built the log cabin he first settled in when arriving in Texas." Everyone who hears this story expresses doubt. "Well," he'd explain, "my grandfather changed the handle because it had started to rot and weaken." After pausing, he would continue. "My father changed the axe-head because it had gotten a bit rusty and wasn't holding an edge. I've sharpened it a lot. To my family, it's the same axe. This new church might have a different handle and a new axe-head, but it's the same church that's been serving Jesus for generations."

After Peter, James lends his support and addresses the inevitable argument that always follows ministry with those who have been oppressed. "If we give up on that rule, it'll be a slippery slope to [insert some other rule]." James holds a line on the essentials (see Acts 15:19)—more, probably, to mollify detractors than to actually give advice to uncircumcised leaders. Without a thorough and specific context, it is hard to know whether Peter offers a compromise that would bother Gentiles or simply a crafty rebuttal to mollify critics, knowing that Gentile church leaders would consider these requirements as nonissues. Either way, this story presents questions for the church of any age: What are the true essentials? What compromises do we make for peace and unity? With whom do we prioritize unity if we need to choose between groups or theologies? What are the real distinctions between uniformity and unity?

Acknowledge Harm and Offer Solidarity

After ruling that circumcision is not necessary for salvation or church leadership, the Jerusalem Council drafted a pastoral letter to Gentile Christians (Acts 15:23-29): "We've heard that some of our number have disturbed you with unsettling words we didn't authorize" (Acts 15:24). However, common English translations lose the significance of the original Greek. The word translated as "disturbed" comes from the Greek *tarassō*, which suggests emotional or mental turmoil. The Greek word for "unsettling" literally translates to "unequipping" or "dismantling." In the fuller context, the phrase could reasonably be translated as "set you into turmoil, dismantling your work and your souls." Before oppressors can become co-conspirators with the oppressed, they must acknowledge the deep harm done by exclusion. Confession must take place before repentance—even if the harm was done by people other than those seeking a stronger relationship with the oppressed.

One of the most striking moments in the Prayer of Confession in the United Methodist communion liturgy is that all our confessions are collective:

Merciful God,
we confess that we have not loved you with our whole hearts.
We have failed to be an obedient church.
We have not done your will,
we have broken your law,
we have rebelled against your love,
we have not loved our neighbors,
and we have not heard the cry of the needy.
Forgive us, we pray.
Free us for joyful obedience,
through Jesus Christ our Lord. Amen.[2]

It is entirely possible that some members of the congregation did not rebel against God's love since they last took Communion. Perhaps some individuals have made obedient decisions in the church. Still, we pray collectively for forgiveness. If we are to share in the work of healing and reconciliation, we must share in the work of confession.

I wonder whether the Jerusalem Council letter would have been more powerful if it had asked the Gentiles for forgiveness rather than just acknowledging the harm done. If the Communion liturgy calls upon us to confess collectively before we individually approach the table, surely collective confession is appropriate should we ever pursue institutional reconciliation. My individual culpability or lack thereof does not matter. I am a part of a body that has done harm, and I bear that responsibility to those whom I wish to offer repair and healing.

The power of the Jerusalem Council's letter (Acts 15:23-29) is its embodiment. Instead of just sending written words to the churches in Antioch, Syria, and Cilicia, the council in Jerusalem sends people—Judas and Silas, in addition to Paul and Barnabas. The letter encourages both those who received it and those who embodied it: "The people read it, delighted with its *encouraging* message. Judas and Silas . . . said many things that *encouraged* and strengthened the brothers and sisters" (Acts 15:31-32, emphasis added).

Here again, a better understanding of Greek is helpful. The Greek word translated as "encouraged" (*parakaleō*) literally means "to call alongside." The Gentile leaders experienced more than just comfort; they experienced solidarity with those who would walk alongside them in mission. Notice that *parakaleō* uses the same root word for the most common honorific given the Holy Spirit: *paraclete*. The Holy Spirit, it seems, shows up when those in power acknowledge harm, offer clear support, and walk alongside the oppressed.

Forsake Privilege

Luke, the author of Acts, does not forsake his privilege in this story. The only time he gives voice to those who have been marginalized is in Acts 15:31-32, when the Gentile leaders receive the letter as an encouragement. They were not invited to the Jerusalem Council—only Paul and Barnabas. The text does not discuss the betrayal—or perhaps full vitriol—the Gentile leaders may have felt knowing that "some people . . . from Judea" (Acts 15:1) questioned their salvation as uncircumcised Christians. While the institutional church demonstrates good work in Acts 15, it is not without fault or room for improvement. May we build upon its successes, finding a more excellent way as the church strives ever on to perfection.

Reflection Questions

1. Which leadership style in ministry with the marginalized are you most likely called to? Peter and James, who offer institutional cover? Paul and Barnabas, who specialize in ministry with the oppressed? Judas and Silas, who walk alongside as institutional representatives?

2. When have you felt that someone has been called alongside you? How do you know when someone offers true solidarity?

3. When have you dismissed advocates who share your identity when they speak truth about communities you don't know well?

4. The Jerusalem Council wrote to Gentile Christians, "Some of our number have disturbed you with unsettling words" (Acts 15:24; more literally, "set you into turmoil, dismantling your work and your souls"). Who needs to hear a similar acknowledgment of harm from your church, denomination, or faith community? How about your employer or government? What would it mean for your community to confess?

5. Is there a value to collective confession even if the person confessing wasn't personally responsible for the harm?

General Conference or Gendered Conference?

Ashley Boggan

The Methodist tradition has always uplifted White, male, heterosexual, ordained men to places of prominence. At various points in our past, if you were anything other than all those adjectives combined, you were a second-class citizen. This was especially heart-wrenching in the late nineteenth century when Methodist women were the backbone of the denomination's mission and witness, and yet they were (repeatedly) denied not only ordination but voice.

In 1888, five laywomen were duly elected by their annual conferences as delegates to the General Conference of The Methodist Episcopal Church—the denomination's highest legislative body. Their elections were legal under the existing *Book of Discipline* language governing lay representation. Yet when they arrived at the General Conference, credentials in hand, they encountered a harsh reality: The church that had relied on women's labor, leadership, and funding for decades was unwilling to recognize them as equals within its own governing life.[3]

The five women—Anna Howard Shaw, Frances Willard, Mary A. Townsend, Mary A. Wright, and Clara C. Hoffman—were not marginal figures. Willard was the internationally known president of the Woman's Christian

Temperance Union. Shaw was an ordained Methodist preacher (later defrocked) and a leading suffragist. The others were prominent lay leaders within their conferences. Their presence embodied the reality that women already sustained The Methodist Episcopal Church through mission societies, education, philanthropy, and evangelism.

Nevertheless, when the General Conference convened, the women were denied seats on the conference floor. Instead, they were relegated to the gallery—physically present but legislatively invisible. Their credentials were challenged, debated, and ultimately rejected. In that moment, the church rendered them second-class citizens: recognized as Methodists and acknowledged as contributors, but not affirmed as authoritative voices.

The debate was not about capability or faithfulness; it was about gender. Opponents argued that "laymen" in the *Book of Discipline* implicitly excluded women, despite the absence of explicit prohibitory language. Others warned that seating women would upend the "natural order" of church governance. The irony was glaring: Methodism's connectional system had long depended on women's organizational leadership, yet it balked at granting women deliberative power.

Within the bar of the conference, however, powerful voices rose in defense of the women's inclusion. Most notably, John P. Newman, presiding bishop at the opening of the General Conference, ruled that the women were lawfully elected and entitled to their seats. His decision was grounded not in novelty but in fairness and fidelity to Methodist polity. According to contemporary accounts, Bishop Newman declared that the General Conference had no authority to impose qualifications not specified by church law, effectively affirming the women's right to participate fully.[4]

Other clergy spoke with equal moral clarity. Leander L. Bowman argued forcefully that the exclusion of women violated both justice and Methodist tradition. In words widely reported in Methodist periodicals, Bowman insisted that there was "no law of God, no law of the church, and no law of common justice" that justified denying women their seats.[5] The issue, he contended, was not custom but conscience.

Support also came from leading pastors and theologians on the floor. James M. Buckley, though later known for opposing women's ordination, acknowledged during the debates that the women had been properly elected and that the church risked grave injustice by excluding them. Others explicitly named the contradiction at the heart of the church's action: Methodism celebrated women as missionaries and moral reformers, yet silenced them when decisions about doctrine, polity, and mission were made.

Despite these arguments, Bishop Newman's ruling was appealed and overturned by the conference. The five women remained excluded.[6] Their treatment sent an unmistakable message: Women could serve but not govern; they could speak but not decide. The pain of that exclusion was compounded by its public nature—enacted not quietly but through parliamentary maneuver and theological rationalization before the whole church.

Yet the story does not end in defeat. The injustice of 1888 galvanized Methodist women and their allies. It exposed the gap between Methodist practice and Methodist principle, between a theology that proclaimed universal grace and a polity that enforced gender hierarchy. The arguments made on behalf of the five laywomen—rooted in law, justice, and Christian conscience—became the foundation for future reforms. In 1904, women were finally granted full lay representation in The Methodist Episcopal Church.

The 1888 General Conference stands as a sobering reminder that progress in the church is rarely linear. It also bears witness to the courage of those who spoke truth within the bar of the conference—and to the women who, even when denied their seats, revealed the moral cost of exclusion. Their presence forced Methodism to confront its own contradictions and, in doing so, helped move the church, however slowly, toward greater faithfulness.

CHAPTER 4
When the World Calls Justice "Upside Down"
(Acts 16:16-40)

Aleze Fulbright
and Mike Baughman

Some biblical stories ignite our curiosity—the best do so as much in the spaces between lines and letters as in any explicit word or lesson. The second half of Acts 16, which recounts Paul and Silas's imprisonment and from which the title of this book comes, is one of those stories. Rather than our typical chapters, we thought we'd break down this story, bit by bit, alternating between us, Mike and Aleze, as we dig into the story. As we ask questions of the text, we thought we'd ask questions of each other and see what insights emerge.

This chapter explores the cost of faithful discipleship. It invites us to sit in tension. It asks us to question not only the cruelty of the empire but also the selective vision of those who claim righteousness. Its story is not just about unjust imprisonment; it is about how power reacts when it is disturbed. It is about who is seen, who is named, who is protected, and who remains invisible, even in stories of liberation. It is about the cost of disruption and the uneven distribution of that cost.

When we disrupt systems that exploit the vulnerable, there are consequences. Paul and those around him learned this lesson. So will we. The question is not whether we will find crosses along the way but whether we are willing to bear them.

Aleze: *This story starts with Paul on the way back to the "place for prayer" led by Lydia (Acts 16:1; see chapter 7). Here, his feminist chops get a workout. Along the way, he encounters someone the text describes as a "slave woman" (Acts 16:16) who followed Paul for days and kept shouting, "These people are servants of the Most High God! They are proclaiming a way of salvation to you!" (Acts 16:17-18). Do you think Lydia would be proud of Paul's response?*

Mike: While Paul does cast out whatever spirit was possessing the woman, I have a feeling that Lydia is the type of boss who sees the big picture and would have scolded Paul right away—and maybe the author of Acts as well. This woman is dehumanized—by the people who dare to enslave her, by customers who seek her fortune-telling and pay those who claim to own her, by the Bible that never names her, and by Paul who "heals" her not out of a desire to offer care but because she "annoyed Paul so much" (Acts 16:18). She is a commodity, a plot point, an annoyance.

I wonder whether Paul thought through what would happen to her when she was no longer valuable to those who enslaved her. Was there an exit strategy? A way for her to support herself? We sometimes talk about "when healing harms," and this may be one of those cases. While many mission trips offer critical support and healing, a great many do more harm than good. They risk turning those who are marginalized into object lessons (emphasis on "object") or minimizing the agency/abilities of those we "travel to serve" by assuming we know better than them how to build a house, educate their children, or navigate their world without doing harm.

Faithful ministry always sees the full personhood of those we serve. Paul creates a catastrophe for himself and the woman he heals, but the text focuses only on his personal fiasco. Her dignity is dismissed and her indignity forgotten. Ironically, Paul later accuses the police of failing to affirm his dignity or inquire about the depths of his privilege (Acts 16:37) and uses this to expose their guilt in this whole affair. If she knew the whole story, I think Lydia is the kind of woman who might get after Paul and tell him to fix the mess he made.

Aleze: *Her enslavers were upset because their "hope for making money was gone" (Acts 16:19). Similarly, in chapter 9, we will see the crowds riled up by concern over how Paul disrupts the local economy. There seems to be a recurring thread of economics that gets Paul and the early church into trouble. What's the cautionary tale here?*

Mike: The Bible is not shy in talking about money. Economic systems, wealth disparity, predatory lending, hoarding, and other financial processes are major topics throughout the Hebrew Bible and New Testament. It's pretty clear that a biblical vision for the world will upend and destabilize any economic system that prioritizes stability and growth over equity and poverty alleviation—especially the current economic system in the United States. I think God does not think economic systems are bad; I think God just thinks *bad* economic systems are bad. Indeed, it seems God lays out the economic system of Jubilee (among others) to ensure that debt never runs too rampant.

Faithfulness to our baptismal vow to "accept the freedom and power God gives you to resist evil, injustice, and oppression in whatever forms they present themselves"[1] will inevitably prioritize equity over economic stability—and that will upset people who benefit from the current system.

Economic systems are not just something to disrupt. Our power in economic systems can be a tool for justice. Wespath, the pension and benefits organization for The United Methodist Church, consistently tells stories of ways it leverages its holdings to influence the practices of international corporations and investors. When boycotts change balance sheets, corporate systems change course. However, these shifts are rarely fast. *The Birmingham bus boycott took 381 days.* New social enterprises take years to impact their local markets, let alone regional ones. Economic systems can be a powerful means of change, but those who use them need to recognize the long struggle required to shift such well-entrenched money and systems.

The enslaved owners were upset because Paul disrupted their economic exploitation. They did not care about the woman. They cared about profits. This is a pattern throughout Acts: People get most upset when Paul disrupts economic systems built upon exploitation.

Mike: *Paul and his disciples are described as "these people who have been turning the world upside down" (Acts 17:6 NRSVue) and "Jews who promote customs that we Romans can't accept or practice" (Acts 16:20b-21). Before we tackle the literal violence of the crowd, what's the significance of calling them "these people" and rejecting their "customs"?*

Aleze: The crowd is incited not by theological debate but by framing: "These men are disturbing our city; they are Jews and are advocating customs that are not lawful for us as Romans to adopt or observe" (Acts 16:20-21, NRSVue). Before the rods strike Paul and Silas, before the prison doors close, violence has already taken place—violence of language, of categorization, the violence of "othering."

"They." "These people." "Not us." This is the oldest strategy of domination. To call someone "these people" is to refuse relational proximity. It is to strip individuals of names, stories, and nuance. More importantly, these phrases do not describe behavior; they construct threat: a perceived threat of danger, a transference of power, and a fear of no longer being in control.

Notice the layering of the accusation. Paul and Silas are not merely disruptive; they are framed as religiously suspect (Jews) and culturally incompatible (their customs). The charge is not that they are wrong, but that they are "other." Their very presence is presented as destabilizing to the social order. The Empire does not fear belief as much as it fears differences that cannot be controlled. The issue here is not that Paul and Silas are spiritual; it is that their message interrupts profit, power, and predictability. The enslaved woman's liberation has already cost her owners economically. What cannot be punished directly is rerouted into a narrative of civic danger.

This is how systemic violence often works. Moral outrage is weaponized selectively. The crowd is not upset that a young woman has been enslaved, exploited, and commodified. They are upset that her exploitation has been interrupted. The real offense is not injustice; it is disruption.

While the biblical example is illuminated here, the contemporary realities are witnessed throughout the chronicles of time. As one who has often been categorized as "other," the painful truth is that often the majority, even in the church, are more concerned about their domination rather than my humanity.

Mike: *Paul's detractors call a world without Paul's influence "upside down." What insight does this have for the church? What does it tell us about how we see the world?*

Aleze: Paul's detractors claim that Paul and his companions are "turning the world upside down" (Acts 17:6, NRSVue). What they mean, of course, is that Paul is disturbing their world—the world as they know it, which they benefit from and presume should remain. What they cannot see is that the world they are defending is already upside down.

This accusation exposes a crucial aspect of perspective. Those at the center of power experience any movement toward justice as chaos. Equity feels like loss when you are accustomed to advantage. Liberation sounds like a threat when your stability depends on someone else's confinement.

For the early church, this accusation became a strange badge of honor. The gospel did not merely save souls; it reordered loyalties. It challenged household codes, economic arrangements, and assumptions about worth. The problem was never that the gospel was too political; it was that it was too honest. The gospel is not interested in being palatable to power; it is interested in being faithful to truth.

The church today must wrestle with this question: Which world are we trying to keep right-side up? Is it the world as God intends, or the world as we have learned to survive within it? This is a challenging question for churches and those within them who have grown comfortable. If our faith never disrupts anything, we must consider what kind of gospel we are proclaiming. The early church did not seek upheaval for its own sake, but neither did it confuse peace with silence. A world that calls justice "upside down" has already revealed its moral orientation. The language of "upside down" reveals fear—not of

God, but of change. It reveals an imagination so captive to the present arrangement that it cannot conceive of holiness apart from hierarchy.

Aleze: *After accusations, the authorities ordered Paul and Silas "be stripped of their clothes and beaten with a rod" (Acts 16:22). They are then thrown in prison and their feet secured in stocks (Acts 16:23-24). What is the significance of this?*

Mike: I'm tired of horror tears. My first memory of horror tears was March 1991, when I saw footage of police officers beating Rodney King. Others have been far closer to my home in Dallas, Texas: Jordan Edwards, Botham Jean, and Breonna Taylor all inspired horror tears, and I know that I am protected from violence in a way that they were not. As recently as the week I'm writing this chapter, I found myself in horror tears again as people died at the hands of federal officers.

While all violence is traumatic, there is something extraordinarily demoralizing about state-sanctioned violence against its own people. The Boston Massacre killed five people—that was enough to spark a revolution against an empire that could no longer claim it cared about the people in the Americas. It takes decades and endless court cases before even the most death penalty–friendly states will execute a person. Whether it's firebombing Black Wall Street, troopers on the Edmund Pettis Bridge, police officers kneeling on the back of George Floyd, or ICE agents terrorizing citizens and immigrants alike, violent acts of injustice on the part of the state break our social contract.

The irony is that violent acts (supposedly done in the name of security) lead most people to feel less safe.

Paul and Silas are victims of state-sanctioned violence. So was Jesus. I do not know how we can worship one victim of state-sanctioned violence on Sunday morning while reading Scripture written by another victim of state-sanctioned violence and ignore these acts the rest of the week.

Aleze: *Paul and Silas pray and sing hymns to God while in prison (Acts 16:25). Why does the Scripture include this detail?*

Mike: There is a magic to communal singing. Our breath literally syncs up with others'—and so does our heartbeat. Physiologically, we feel less alone. As I write this chapter, fresh horrors keep emerging from ICE-related events in Minneapolis, but so too do TikTok reel after TikTok reel of protestors singing! Their harmonies seem powered by old memories of the Lutheran churches that many of the protestors no longer attend but still provide a source of strength. Civil rights movements in America, Ireland, Palestine, South Africa, and beyond share a common attention to song. It connects us not only with one another but also, across time, to the strength of those who have run the marathons of justice.

I suspect that Paul and Silas sing for courage and comfort, for healing and hope. They sing to bridge the divide between one another, between prisoners in disconnected cells, and between them and the God they serve, who may seem distant but dwells in the songs they've sung for generations.

Mike: *Paul and Silas are really nice to their jailer. Despite their earlier failure to consider the humanity of the enslaved woman, they see the jailer's full humanity and the consequences of their actions. Given that Paul and Silas were less than helpful with the enslaved woman, what lessons can we learn from their interactions with the jailer?*

Aleze: One of the most unsettling aspects of Acts 16 is the contrast between Paul and Silas's interaction with the enslaved woman and their interaction with the jailer. The woman's liberation is almost incidental.

Paul is annoyed. Her humanity is secondary to the disruption she causes. The text does not linger on her fate once the spirit is cast out. We are left to wonder what freedom actually looked like for her in a society that had already marked her as property and less than.

With the jailer, however, the narrative slows. Paul and Silas notice his despair and intervene to save his life (Acts 16:27-28). They speak to him with tenderness and accept his hospitality; his family is baptized, and his humanity is fully affirmed (Acts 16:31-34).

This contrast should trouble us—not because Paul and Silas are villains but because even apostles have blind spots. Even liberation movements can replicate harm when they fail to center the most vulnerable.

Mike: *Paul endures terrible pain through this and so many other stories. Can you speak to the cost that comes with being a co-conspirator with the oppressed?*

Aleze: Paul's suffering in this passage is real. He is beaten publicly, imprisoned unjustly, and humiliated without due process. This is not metaphorical discomfort; it is bodily harm. And it comes not because he is reckless but because he has aligned himself, even imperfectly, with a movement that threatens entrenched power.

To be a co-conspirator with the oppressed is costly. It costs reputation. It costs security. It often costs relationships. Sometimes it costs physical safety. And for people categorized as "other," these costs trigger personal and ancestral trauma. These truths are what the church must reclaim without romanticizing suffering.

Paul does not seek pain, but he accepts it as part of discipleship. His suffering is not salvific in itself; it is consequential. Paul eventually invokes his Roman citizenship. He demands accountability. He leaves the city with his dignity publicly restored. The same system that brutalized him is forced to apologize. Paul can endure suffering in part because he knows it is not the end of the story. He has an escape clause that many do not.

Suffering happens when truth collides with power. Yet even here, we cannot dismiss that privilege complicates the story. Privilege does not eliminate suffering, but it shapes its limits. To be a co-conspirator is not simply to endure pain; it is to leverage whatever privilege one has for the sake of those without privilege. Paul does this imperfectly but intentionally. His insistence on public accountability is not about ego; it is about protection for the fledgling community he leaves behind.

Mike: When we divest our privilege to invest in equity, there is almost always a price. Renee Good spoke on behalf of immigrants, and Alex Pretti advocated for a woman who was pepper-sprayed on the street. They let go of their privilege and, therefore, the protections it affords. Oppressive voices quickly sought to discredit them and concoct stories to disparage the victims. Divesting privilege does not always lead to death, but it commonly comes with consequences—jobs lost, poor performance reviews, fewer donations, and lost friendships, to name a few. And here's a hard truth: Sometimes we make our best efforts at equity, taking our hits, and still we do not have the impact we thought we would. Each act of resistance is a seed. Every act of equity bends the arc of the universe ever so slightly more toward justice. We may not see the harvest, but we plant anyway and trust that God will cultivate hope in whatever dark soil we find. The simple truth is that crosses come with consequences, but in losing our lives for Christ, we will find true life.

Aleze: The Book of Acts does not present Paul as a flawless hero, nor does it condemn him as a hypocrite. It presents him as a man being transformed in public, navigating the tension between conviction and context, courage and complication. Privilege, as we see it in Acts, is neither wholly rejected nor uncritically embraced. It is a tool—dangerous if ignored but powerful if surrendered to God's purposes.

The gospel has always been unsettling. It refuses to leave systems untouched or hearts unchanged. It calls us not merely to sympathy but to solidarity, not merely to belief but to embodied risk. Paul's story, in all its brilliance and blemish, reminds us that faithfulness is not about perfection. It is about willingness to be disrupted, to be corrected, and to be used by God even as we are still being shaped.

This deep reflection on Paul's story invites us and the church to examine not only what we believe but also how our location shapes our witness. This reading of Acts prompts us to examine whom we see and whom we overlook. We must ask ourselves: Which worlds are we trying to keep right-side up? Additionally, if the early church was accused of turning the world upside down, perhaps the modern church should consider whether we have become too invested in keeping it exactly as it is.

And perhaps that is the quiet invitation of Acts—not to admire Paul from a distance but to examine ourselves up close, asking whether we are prepared, truly prepared, for the cost of turning a broken world right-side up again.

Reflection Questions

1. The enslaved woman is liberated from spiritual oppression but remains vulnerable within a social system that profits from her harm. Where do you see partial justice at work today, when liberation stops short of full restoration?

2. How might Acts 16:16-40 be different if Paul had seen and honored the woman's humanity?

3. What customs or traditions (in church, culture, politics) do you find yourself defending most directly? How might those customs be shielding systems that the gospel calls into question?

4. When else in history or contemporary society have you seen economic disruption lead to either violence or positive social change?

5. What costs have you paid for equity?

6. Who are the people whose suffering has become so normalized that you rarely notice it anymore? What practices might help reawaken your attention and compassion?

7. If someone were to accuse you or your ministry setting of turning the world upside down, what evidence might they point to? What evidence is missing?

Always Look a Mob in the Face

Ashley Boggan

In the autumn of 1742, Charles Wesley preached the gospel on a simple hillside at Wednesbury in Staffordshire, England, marking one of the earliest forays of Methodism into the rough industrial Black Country. Within months, a society of more than three hundred believers had formed, invigorated by the Wesley brothers' message of personal holiness, social transformation, and the immediate experience of God's saving grace. Yet this burgeoning community encountered fierce opposition—much of it erupting in violent mobs that sought to silence and intimidate the Methodists.

The hostility at Wednesbury was not random. The industrial towns of Wednesbury, Walsall, and Darlaston were notorious for their lawless character, where bull-baiting, cockfighting, and open confrontation were part of local entertainment and identity. Into that milieu came itinerant preachers whose message undermined more than religious complacency: Wesleyan evangelism challenged social hierarchies, advocated a disciplined ethic for the poor, and preached equality before God in an age of entrenched class privilege.

When John Wesley arrived later that year to support the local society, the tension exploded into violence. A mob beset him outside Francis Ward's house, crying for the preacher's removal. Wesley himself later recorded the scene: Men tried to seize him by the collar, and blows rained down—one splitting his mouth and another hitting his breast so that blood flowed. Yet amid the chaos, Wesley maintained "as much presence of mind as if he had been sitting in his study."[2]

At one point, as the mob howled with murderous intent—some shouting "Down with him! Kill him at once!"—Wesley stood in the center of the tumult and asked if they "were willing to hear me speak."[3] A faction of the crowd momentarily stilled, and Wesley prayed aloud. Even the ruffian who had led the attack turned and vowed to protect him, and others followed, ultimately escorting Wesley back to safety.

This incident was not an isolated anomaly but part of a broader pattern of resistance to Methodist preaching. Clergy hostile to the movement actively inflamed local passions; at one point, the vicar of Wednesbury encouraged parishioners to pledge not to associate with Methodists—a pledge that, when refused, resulted in smashed windows and destroyed furniture for those sympathetic to the Wesleys. And it was not only directed at John. Charles, his brother, also faced physical opposition, usually in the same region. In 1743, Charles visited Wednesbury and began gathering the three hundred society members. As they walked toward the preacher's house, they sang. As they reached the meeting house, an angry mob awaited them and shouted a quote from Acts 17:6: "Behold, they that turn the world upside down are come here also" (Acts 17:6, KJV). *They that turn the world upside down. Those people called Methodist, who turn the world upside down, have come here also.* Charles, in a similar fashion to John, refused to be silenced by the mob. He stepped up on the market square and began preaching and singing. With every punch thrown his way, he sang louder, blessing those who beat him.[4]

The mobs that assailed John and Charles Wesley were motivated by more than mere theological disagreement. Their violence reflected a profound discomfort with the ways in which Methodist preaching critiqued social norms: the entrenched class order, the indifference of established religion to moral and economic injustice, and the message that the gospel demanded both inner holiness and practical justice. Many commentators have noted that Methodist teaching, particularly its emphasis on the new birth and the holiness of life, appeared unsettling and even dangerously enthusiastic to skeptical observers.

The image of Methodist gatherings turning the world upside down was not hyperbole but a lived reality—indeed, critics often accused them of exactly that. Their open-air preaching drew workers away from taverns, their insistence on moral accountability threatened entrenched patterns of labor and leisure, and their egalitarian emphasis challenged rigid class boundaries in provincial England. No surprise, then, that mobs gathered, threatened, stoned, and beat them and that justices of the peace sometimes refused even to investigate.

This pattern of opposition, suffering, and steadfast witness resonates with many of Paul's experiences. In Acts 21 and 22, Paul was dragged from the temple by an enraged mob; cries of "Kill him!" (Acts 21:36) followed him up the steps until Roman soldiers intervened and carried him for protection. Earlier, in Ephesus, crowds incited by economic anxiety over the threatened idol business near the theater rioted for hours, shouting against Paul's message.

Both Wesley and Paul faced resistance rooted in the ways their preaching disrupted familiar social structures. Paul's proclamation that Gentiles and Jews were both heirs of God's promises destabilized first-century boundaries of ethnicity, religion, and honor. Similarly, the Wesley brothers' preaching destabilized eighteenth-century British class hierarchies and the complacency of an established church content with its social privileges.

But the parallel goes deeper than disruption. In Acts, Paul's imprisonment and beatings were anticipated consequences of his obedience—as the risen Christ told him earlier, he would suffer for the sake of the gospel. Likewise, John Wesley understood persecution and mob violence not as aberrations but as inherent to a gospel that upended religious formalism and moral indifference. In his own journal, Wesley remarked that he would never fear mobs; he would "always look a mob in the face," trusting that divine providence was at work even amid threats of violence.[5]

In both the early church and the Methodist revival, we see a similar pattern: *A message that unsettles the world will incite resistance, yet faithfulness unto suffering becomes a powerful witness.* Paul's eventual imprisonment in Rome did not silence the gospel; it amplified it. The mob hostility that greeted the Wesleys at Wednesbury did not prevent Methodism's spread; it underscored the moral urgency of their critique of class, economics, and religion in Georgian England.

In these testimonies—of Paul in Acts and the Wesleys in Staffordshire—there echoes a basic truth of Christian witness: The good news that confronts human complacency and injustice will always carry the risk of backlash. The Wesley account reminds us that steadfast courage, rooted in conviction and guided by love, has the power not only to endure persecution but also to transform even its fiercest opponents into allies of the gospel.

CHAPTER 5
Big Church Energy and Financial Privilege
Paul, Tentmaking, and the Freedom to Speak Truth (Acts 18; 24)

Aleze Fulbright

In chapter 1, we explored how Saul of Tarsus was formed by layers of advantage, such as education under Gamaliel, Roman citizenship, male status, religious authority, and social standing, which positioned him to move through the first-century world with remarkable access and credibility. Saul's privilege did not negate his suffering, nor did it guarantee moral clarity. Instead, it shaped how he interpreted the world, exercised power, and understood his own righteousness.

There is a certain confidence that emerges when a preacher knows the rent is paid, the lights are on, and tomorrow's bread is not in jeopardy. That confidence is not arrogance; it is freedom—the ability to speak boldly because one is not immediately vulnerable to retaliation, termination, or starvation. But long before megachurches, endowments, or denominational guarantees, the apostle Paul embodied a version of this reality through his work as a tentmaker.

Acts 18 and 24 offer us a lens into Paul's ministry that is often, I believe, underdeveloped in theological reflection: the role of financial independence as a form of privilege that enables prophetic courage. Paul's tentmaking vocation was not merely a biographical detail; it was a theological strategy. His ability to fund his own ministry gave him freedom to confront synagogue leaders, Roman authorities, and wealthy patrons without fear of losing his livelihood. Paul's citizenship protects him from certain abuses, but now we see another form of privilege operating quietly beneath the surface: financial independence. That freedom shaped both what he said and how he said it. I approach this text with reverence for Paul's ingenuity and realism about how privilege operates unevenly across race, gender, and institutional power in both ancient and modern contexts. I read Paul's story with both gratitude and interrogation—gratitude for the freedom his model imagines and interrogation for the ways privilege still determines who gets to be bold without being broken.

This chapter argues that Paul's financial autonomy is a form of privilege that, when rightly stewarded, can be leveraged for truth-telling and systemic change but, when misunderstood or ignored, can distort ministry practice and silence prophetic witness. Paul's work was an economic extension of Saul's earlier privilege, granting him the freedom to speak truth to religious and political power without the immediate threat of starvation or termination. This kind of independence, which I name here as "big church energy," is not about arrogance or size; it is about capacity—the capacity to risk honestly.

Tentmaking as Theological Praxis

In chapter 1, we saw that Saul's formation occurred in elite spaces—in Jerusalem classrooms, among synagogue leadership, and within networks of authority. However, Acts 18 introduces Paul in Corinth, one of the most economically stratified and morally complex cities of the Roman Empire. Luke tells us that Paul stayed with Aquila and Priscilla, "and, because he was of the same trade, he stayed with them, and they worked together—by trade they were tentmakers" (Acts 18:3, NRSVue).

Paul is no longer primarily teaching in halls of prestige. He is working with his hands. It was not glamorous work. Manual labor was often associated with lower social status, even though skilled artisans could earn a stable income.[1] Paul's choice to work was not accidental. His vocational independence served a strategic purpose in a city like Corinth, where patronage systems threatened to entangle preachers in obligations to wealthy benefactors.[2] Engaging in manual labor is not a contradiction of Saul's privilege; it is its reconfiguration. Paul's ability to oscillate between synagogue debates and manual labor placed him in multiple social worlds simultaneously. So, by funding his own ministry, Paul refused to become beholden to elite donors who might expect theological compromise in exchange for financial support. This independence allowed Paul to proclaim a gospel that challenged social hierarchies rather than reinforcing them. This dual positioning gave Paul rare flexibility, where he could critique systems without being fully captive to them.

Privilege Defined

Privilege is often misunderstood as wealth alone. In reality, privilege is best understood as the capacity to absorb risk without catastrophic loss. Paul's tentmaking enabled him to take risks, confront synagogue leaders, challenge Roman officials, and leave hostile cities without immediately endangering his survival. This distinction matters. Paul was not wealthy by Roman standards, but he had enough resources to move freely. He had education, literacy, Roman citizenship, vocational skills, and social networks. Together, these assets constituted a form of privilege that allowed him to operate with remarkable boldness.

Paul himself acknowledges this dynamic when he tells the Corinthians, "We have not made use of this right, but we endure anything rather than put an obstacle in the way of the gospel of Christ" (1 Corinthians 9:12, NRSVue). His refusal to accept financial support was a conscious theological choice shaped by his ability to provide for himself. This refusal mattered because it was a choice, and choice is the clearest marker of privilege. Paul's courage is not only theological; it is also structural.

Acts 24 places Paul before Governor Felix, a Roman official with both political authority and moral corruption. Paul stands accused by religious leaders who view his movement as a threat to public order. Yet Paul does not grovel. He speaks calmly, confidently, and unapologetically about justice, self-control, and the coming judgment (Acts 24:24-25). What allows this posture?

Paul's boldness is often attributed to his faith alone, but faith operates within material realities. Paul is not dependent on Felix for employment. He is not angling for patronage. His survival does not hinge on pleasing Roman authorities. His tentmaking ministry, combined with support from other churches when appropriate, insulated him from immediate economic coercion (Philippians 4:15-16). This matters deeply for contemporary ministry. Too often, prophetic silence is explained away as prudence when it is actually a matter of economic fear. When preachers' livelihoods are entirely controlled by those they are called to challenge, the gospel is inevitably muted.

I think about an array of examples, as I formerly served as a district superintendent and received an inordinate number of emails because a pastor decided to preach what Rev. Dr. Frank Thomas calls "a dangerous sermon."[3] His message was steeped in biblical witness and spoke to current injustices. The complaints made were extreme, simply because the message moved people beyond their comfort and into being deployed as followers of Jesus Christ into the world. I would also suggest that if these messages were delivered by those in cross-racial, cross-cultural appointments, the discomfort would become even more apparent. There would be a rally for a "vote of no confidence," or, if these challenges had become compounded, the people would hold fast to the belief that an appointment change was imperative. This is the current reality for many, being afraid to speak what "thus saith the Lord" for fear of what "thus saith the uncomfortable people."

And so, I read Paul's account with both admiration and caution as Paul's freedom to choose independence is itself a privilege not universally available, especially to those historically excluded from economic stability or institutional protection. As the contemporary clergy know all too well, one sermon, one protest, or one pastoral stand could cost them housing, health care, or retirement. Even as I acknowledge my own points of privilege, I know there is a limitation to how and where I speak. I often imagine a time and space where I will no longer feel scared of retribution, and I wonder, *What does this freedom truly resemble for those who look like me?*

Independence and Accountability

Paul's financial independence did not make him a rogue operator. The issue was not money itself but control. This tension remains alive in modern ministry. Financial independence can empower prophetic speech, but it can also foster isolation, arrogance, or a lack of accountability. Paul models a balance: autonomy without detachment, freedom without individualism.

African American church history offers striking parallels to Paul's tentmaking theology. Enslaved and formerly enslaved Black preachers often worked multiple jobs—farming, teaching, and skilled trades—so they could preach without White oversight.[4] Economic self-sufficiency enabled theological autonomy. The movement's leaders, such as Richard Allen, the founder of the African Methodist Episcopal Church, understood that financial independence was essential for spiritual freedom. Allen's insistence on Black-controlled worship spaces was inseparable from economic self-governance.[5] In predominantly White Methodist contexts, institutional privilege enabled clergy to advocate for labor reforms, child labor laws, and economic justice during the early twentieth century.[6] Yet that same privilege often excluded Black voices and constrained how far critiques of racism could go. Privilege, once again, proved double-edged: it created platforms for justice while simultaneously reinforcing racial hierarchies.

In the modern United Methodist Church, financial privilege continues to shape whose voices carry weight. Clergy with pensions, endowments, or alternative income streams are often more willing to challenge denominational policies than those living appointment to appointment.

Recent debates over LGBTQ+ inclusion, racial justice, and denominational restructuring reveal how economic security, in my opinion, influences prophetic risk-taking. Those with less to lose can speak more freely; those without safety nets often bear the greatest cost. "Big church energy" is not about megachurches; it is about margin. Margin creates mobility. Mobility creates courage. Paul's story challenges denominational leaders to ask: Who has margin? Who doesn't? And why? The challenge for today's church, especially within historically powerful institutions, is not whether we have privilege but whether we are willing to spend it.

Conclusion

Paul's tentmaking invites a pressing question: What are we doing with the privilege we have? Privilege does not automatically produce justice; it must be intentionally stewarded. For those of us with educational credentials, institutional backing, or financial stability, Paul's example calls us to leverage these assets for the sake of truth, not comfort. Silence in the face of injustice is not neutrality; it is a misuse of privilege. Paul's ministry in Acts 18 and 24 reminds us that courage is not only spiritual but also structural. The freedom to speak truth to power is shaped by economic realities, vocational choices, and institutional positioning.

I read Paul's story as both an inspiration and a challenge. It invites us to ask hard questions about who gets to be brave, who pays the price for honesty, and how the church might cultivate conditions where truth-telling is not economically suicidal. Paul's tentmaking was not a retreat from ministry; it was an expansion of it. May we, too, find ways to integrate our labor, privilege, and prophetic calling so that the gospel we proclaim is as free as the Christ we follow.

Reflection Questions

1. Paul's tentmaking gave him the capacity to absorb risk without catastrophic loss. Consider your capacity to absorb risk: Could you risk speaking truth to power, take a professional hit, and still be okay financially? Could you challenge leadership without losing health care, housing, or retirement? To what degree should those answers influence one's outspokenness in the face of injustice?

2. In what ways can cultural privilege justify itself as theological conviction? How can leaders discern the difference in themselves?

3. Aleze suggests that Paul refuses to weaponize truth. What are contemporary examples of truth being used as a weapon rather than a witness?

4. Aleze writes, "Too often, prophetic silence is explained away as prudence when it is actually economic fear." When have you remained silent, not because it was wise but because you feared consequence?

5. Are there effective ways to "speak truth to power" even if you are financially dependent on those in power who, you think, might be bothered by the things you say? Can there be a symbiotic relationship between big donors and prophetic truth-tellers?

6. Paul's financial independence was itself a form of privilege. He had vocational and organizational skills, literacy, and networks, and he could talk to strangers. Somehow, he still had time for a side hustle while leading churches and writing letters! Few people can meet the demands of ministry *and* have energy or time left for a side hustle to establish financial independence. How can churches and denominations create support structures for prophetic leaders who lack Paul's economic tentmaking resources?

7. Paul preached to audiences who were physically present. New technologies now allow us to communicate across space. In what ways has technology, especially social media platforms, shaped the way Christians speak about faith, justice, and morality?

Big Widow Energy

Ashley Boggan

The story of Paul's "big church energy" brings to mind the story of the financier of Methodism, a woman named Selina Shirley, who would become Selina, the Countess of Huntingdon, and would later be known as "Queen of the Methodists."[7] She married Theophilus Hastings, the Earl of Huntingdon (of Robin Hood fame), and counted among her friends King George II, Sarah Churchill, and Lady Mary Wortley Montague. Not only through marriage but also through her upbringing, Selina had financial independence. In her late twenties, Selina was converted through a friend who had been converted by the Wesley brothers. In this era, being "Methodist" or associating with those people called Methodist was a guaranteed way to get kicked out of the aristocracy (or, as the TV show *Bridgerton* calls it, "the ton"). Selina is one of the few people who managed to maintain the balance between status within the upper elite and Methodism. She even went so far as to dare to border on preaching herself. In a letter to Charles Wesley, she stated, "For the past two weeks, I have given instruction and some short exhortations to the weak, and have found them to be of great use, especially among my work people, with whom I spend a part of every day."[8] Widowed at the age of thirty-nine, she found herself the countess of a large estate.

Unfortunately for John and Charles Wesley, just after the countess was widowed, during the 1770s, a rift developed between the Wesleys and George Whitefield. Selina preferred Whitefield's Calvinist-leaning message and would later fund *his version* of Methodism. She named George Whitefield "chaplain," indicating that his ministry from then on was privately funded, not state-funded, and he would go on to call her a "Methodist Archibishop."[9] However, by 1779, she would use her financial independence to declare herself and those who followed Whitefield to be "dissenters." In 1783, she founded the Countess of Huntingdon's Connexion, a dissenting society that followed a more Calvinist interpretation of Methodism. By the time she died at eighty-three, she had financed sixty-four chapels independently and contributed to a few dozen more. She supported Methodist efforts throughout Britain for over fifty years, contributing an estimated £100,000 (£1 million today). And while her theological preferences are not of this historian's preferred leanings, Selina did consistently attend to the poor, and caring for them is part of her legacy.

Selina would have lived a lovely life without associating with those people called Methodist, but that is not where God called her. She not only used her privilege to support the White male Methodist preachers, but she also used her privilege to bring persons of her own class and status to Methodism, to awaken them to the need of those "below them." She also preached what she practiced—literally. During a time when a woman preaching was scandalous beyond all belief, she risked it. And then she even practiced what she preached and ensured that her legacy would benefit women and children beyond her own lifetime. Here, she shows that she was able to critique the Church of England and the state that set her up for financial independence without having her livelihood threatened. Much like Paul, Selina had privilege; she had the capacity to absorb risk without catastrophic loss and chose to use it to finance the Methodist movement.

CHAPTER 6

Paul's Witness in Athens, Part 1

Cultural Privilege and the Way of Wisdom (Acts 17:16-34)

Aleze Fulbright

There are moments when truth must be shouted because silence would be sin. And then there are moments when truth must be translated because shouting only hardens hearts that are already closed. Acts 17:16-34 situates the apostle Paul squarely in one of those latter moments. In Athens, the intellectual, philosophical, and cultural crossroads of the ancient world, Paul demonstrates that unrestrained judgment and abrasive truth-telling rarely move people toward transformation. Instead, wisdom, discernment, and spiritual intelligence are required to invite people into what Scripture calls "a more excellent way" (1 Corinthians 12:31, KJV).

This passage is especially instructive for the contemporary church in the United States, where public discourse has become increasingly polarized, performative, and reactionary. We are living in a cultural moment that often confuses volume with authority and bluntness with faithfulness. Yet Paul's witness in Athens reminds us that truth divorced from wisdom becomes noise, and noise, no matter how righteous it sounds, seldom bears fruit.

I read Acts 17 not merely as an apologetic model but as a pastoral text, one that examines how cultural privilege operates, how power circulates in public discourse, and how the gospel can be proclaimed faithfully without becoming captive to either cultural domination or cultural appeasement. I also read this text as one who is serving in a society shaped by layered histories of exclusion, resistance, and resilience. In this chapter, I suggest Paul's witness in Athens demonstrates how cultural privilege, identity politics, and extreme moralism often derail the very gospel witness we intend to advance.

Cultural Privilege and the Limits of Unfiltered Truth

Luke introduces Athens as a city "full of idols," a phrase that conveys both religious abundance and spiritual fragmentation (Acts 17:16, NRSVue). Paul's spirit is "deeply distressed" as he surveys the landscape (v. 16). This distress is not the irritation of a moral scold; it is the grief of a shepherd who sees people searching for meaning in places that cannot sustain life. Athens was not hostile to new ideas. On the contrary, Luke tells us that Athenians and resident foreigners spent "their time in nothing but telling or hearing something new"

(Acts 17:21, NRSVue). This is not a closed society; it is an open marketplace full of ideas. But openness does not equal receptivity. A culture can be curious without being convertible, tolerant without being transformed. Paul recognizes this tension. Rather than staging a prophetic confrontation in the streets, he engages the Athenians in conversation in the synagogue, in the marketplace, and eventually at the Areopagus. His approach signals a critical pastoral insight: Not every environment requires the same rhetorical strategy. The gospel is unchanging, but its proclamation must be contextually wise.

Paul's encounter with Epicurean and Stoic philosophers exposes the dynamics of cultural privilege at work. These philosophers occupied respected positions within Athenian society. Their frameworks shaped what counted as reasonable, credible, and worth hearing. Paul enters their space as an outsider—a Jew, a foreigner, a preacher of resurrection in a culture suspicious of bodily claims. Yet Paul does not attempt to overpower them with spiritual bravado. He does not mock their idols publicly or shame their ignorance. Instead, he listens long enough to understand their assumptions and then speaks with precision into their worldview.

This restraint is instructive for our present moment. In the United States, many Christians mistake cultural access for spiritual authority. Platforms are confused with callings. Privilege—whether racial, economic, theological, or ideological—often shapes not only what we say but how we say it. When truth is delivered without awareness of power dynamics, it often reinforces harm rather than healing it. The danger Paul avoids in Athens is one the contemporary church regularly embraces: the belief that public confrontation equals prophetic faithfulness. In the United States, truth-telling has increasingly become a performance rather than a pastoral practice. Volume is mistaken for virtue. Certainty is mistaken for courage.

Sociologist and pastor Dr. James Davison Hunter names this dynamic clearly when he argues that modern culture wars are less about moral persuasion and more about "the will to power."[1] When Christian speech is driven by dominance rather than discipleship, it ceases to be witness and becomes spectacle. The gospel is no longer proclaimed; it is brandished.

We have seen this repeatedly in recent years, particularly in the church's public engagement with racial justice. Following the public lynching of George Floyd in 2020, many Christian leaders rushed to make statements. Some spoke with humility and historical awareness, grounding their words in Scripture's long arc toward justice. Others responded defensively, framing calls for racial accountability as threats to orthodoxy or national identity. Then there were others who wanted to speak but were crippled by fear that their voices and perspectives would get lost in the noise of the loudest or those able to "scratch" the ears of listeners.

Dr. Jemar Tisby observed that much of this resistance stemmed not from theological disagreement but from discomfort caused by losing cultural control. "When you're accustomed to privilege," he writes, "equality feels like oppression."[2] That insight names a painful truth: Cultural privilege often disguises itself as theological conviction. Paul does not confuse the two. Though deeply provoked by Athenian idolatry, he refuses to leverage moral outrage as a substitute for wisdom. Recent history bears this out. In debates around racial justice, public health, sexuality, immigration, and political allegiance, the church has frequently defaulted to pronouncement rather than pastoral presence. The result has been widespread disillusionment, especially among younger generations who experience Christian speech as combative rather than compassionate, certain rather than curious.

Paul shows us another way.

Wisdom as Witness

Paul's restraint stands in sharp contrast to much of contemporary Christian discourse, particularly in digital spaces. Social media has flattened theological reflection into slogans and rewarded outrage over understanding. The result has been a generation increasingly suspicious of Christianity, not because they have rejected Christ or the message of Christ but because they have experienced Christians as careless with words, dangerous with actions, and indifferent to impact. A 2016 Pew Research Center study found that among religiously unaffiliated Americans, a significant percentage cited judgmental attitudes and hypocrisy as primary reasons for disengaging from the church.[3]

Truth must be embodied, not abandoned or merely announced. Paul's address at the Areopagus embodies this distinction. He speaks of repentance and judgment, but only after he establishes relational credibility. He does not begin with what the Athenians are doing wrong; he begins with what they are already seeking. Contrast this approach with the way many churches have addressed issues of sexuality and gender identity in recent decades. Even when theological convictions are sincerely held, the manner of communication has often lacked pastoral care. Former evangelical and now theologian Kristin Kobes Du Mez notes that Christian certainty, when untethered from humility, can become "a form of moral arrogance that mistakes rigidity for faithfulness."[4]

Paul models something far more demanding: the discipline of discernment. Standing before the Areopagus, Paul begins not with accusation but with observation: "Athenians, I see how extremely spiritual you are in every way" (Acts 17:22, NRSVue). This is not flattery; it is discernment. Paul names what is true without mocking what is incomplete. He then references an altar "to an unknown god," using their own religious impulse as a bridge to revelation (Acts 17:23, NRSVue). Rather than dismissing their search, Paul dignifies it and then redirects it.

This action is theologically rich and pastorally sophisticated. Paul affirms that human beings are meaning-makers, seekers of transcendence. Yet he also insists that God is not contained by temples, philosophies, or cultural systems. God is both near and other, intimate and sovereign (Acts 17:24-28). Only after establishing common ground does Paul speak of repentance and judgment. Even then, he does so without theatrics. Judgment is presented not as a threat but as an invitation to accountability grounded in resurrection hope (Acts 17:30-31). Some respond with curiosity. Some mock. A few believe (Acts 17:32-34). Luke offers no illusion of mass conversion. Faithfulness, not numbers, is the measure of success here.

Paul's restraint should not be confused with accommodation. He does not dilute the gospel. He proclaims resurrection, a claim that offends both Epicurean materialism and Stoic rationalism. What Paul refuses to do is weaponize truth for the sake of dominance. This distinction matters deeply today. The church is often tempted either to soften the gospel until it is unrecognizable or to harden it into a blunt instrument.

Acts 17 offers a third way: truth spoken with wisdom, courage shaped by love, conviction held with humility. I am keenly aware that wisdom has often been dismissed as weakness, especially when it comes from marginalized voices. Yet Scripture consistently names wisdom as strength. Proverbs teaches that wisdom cries out in the streets, not to shame but to summon. The Book of James reminds us that wisdom from above is "pure, then peaceable, gentle, willing to yield, full of mercy" (James 3:17, NRSVue). Paul embodies this wisdom in Athens.

Contemporary Parallels in the United States

Athens was pluralistic, intellectually curious, and spiritually restless, much like the United States today. We pride ourselves on openness, yet we often lack the patience required for genuine transformation. We want answers without apprenticeship, convictions without formation.

Theologian Willie James Jennings argues that modern Western Christianity has too often been shaped by "theologies of possession" rather than practices of love.[5] When faith is used to secure identity, territory, or superiority, it loses its cruciform shape. This helps explain why blunt truth-telling so often fails in contemporary America. In an open marketplace of ideas, people are not persuaded by force; they are drawn by coherence, credibility, and care. Paul understands this intuitively. He refuses to ridicule Athenian culture, even while exposing its insufficiency. For the BIPOC (Black, Indigenous, people of color) pastors I am in conversation and in community with, this lesson carries added weight. Our communities have long known what it means to have truth shouted at us without love, law without justice, doctrine without dignity. The Black church's prophetic tradition has always held together truth and tenderness, resistance and redemption. That tradition stands much closer to Paul in Athens than to modern Christian culture warriors.

Our cultural moment mirrors Athens more than Jerusalem. We are pluralistic, argumentative, spiritually curious, and deeply divided. Moral certainty abounds, but moral formation is scarce. In recent years, the church's public witness has been repeatedly tested by racial reckoning, political polarization, and social upheaval. In too many cases, Christian speech has sounded more like cultural combat than gospel proclamation. Truth has been shouted without being shepherded. Acts 17 challenges us to ask hard questions:

- Are we more invested in being right than in being redemptive?
- Do our words invite reflection or provoke defensiveness?
- Are we speaking from woundedness or from wisdom?

Paul reminds us that how we speak often determines whether we are heard.

Additionally, I believe three lessons emerge from Paul's witness in Athens. First, begin with listening. Paul observes before he speaks. He intentionally studies the culture. He takes the city's spiritual temperature. Faithful witness requires disciplined attention. Second, name truth without contempt. Paul critiques idolatry without insulting idolaters. He addresses sin without denying dignity. This balance is desperately needed in contemporary Christian discourse. And lastly, trust the Spirit with the results. Paul does not manipulate outcomes. Some believe; others do not. The work of conversion belongs to God.

Conclusion: The Way of Wisdom

Wisdom is often caricatured as compromise. But Scripture tells a different story. Wisdom is costly. It requires restraint when outrage would feel justified. It requires patience when condemnation would seem more expedient. It requires faith that God's Spirit can do what coercion never will. Paul leaves the Areopagus without applause, without institutional power, and without cultural dominance. Yet Luke records that some believed. That is enough.

Faithfulness is not measured by how loudly truth is declared, but by whether love accompanies it. In a society addicted to immediacy and spectacle, the church must recover wisdom as a spiritual discipline. Wisdom slows us down. Wisdom forces us to ask not only, "Is this true?" but also, "Is this necessary? Is this loving? Is this the right moment?" That is not silence. That is maturity.

Acts 17 does not offer a formula for cultural engagement. It offers a posture. Paul stands in Athens neither as a conqueror nor as a coward but as a witness, confident in the gospel, attentive to context, and committed to speaking truth in love. In a world that rewards outrage and punishes nuance, the church must recover the way of wisdom. Wisdom does not abandon conviction. It refines it. It recognizes that transformation rarely happens through humiliation but often begins with invitation.

May we, like Paul, learn to proclaim Christ in ways that are faithful to Scripture, attentive to culture, and anchored in the deep confidence that God is already at work, even in the most crowded marketplaces of ideas.

Reflection Questions

1. Paul was "deeply distressed" by Athenian idols but chose to engage rather than denounce (Acts 17:16, NRSVue). When have you felt deeply distressed by cultural, political, or religious practices different from your own? In what practical ways can you suspend judgment and initially respond with curiosity?

2. Aleze argues, "When truth is delivered without awareness of power dynamics, it often reinforces harm rather than heals it." Have you spoken truth but failed to consider your own power in the room? Have others hurt you when they did not consider their own power? What was the impact? What lessons did you learn?

3. Aleze observes, "Faithfulness is not measured by how loudly truth is declared, but by whether love accompanies it." How have you seen love communicated in ways that opened people up to a connection with the church?

4. How would you describe the traits of "the way of wisdom" for those who wish to have an impact on their community?

Finding God in a Gay Bar

Ashley Boggan

In the early 1960s, a small group of Methodist clergy in San Francisco made a decision that would reverberate far beyond their own denomination. Rather than speaking *about* homosexual persons from the safety of pulpits and committee rooms, they chose to speak *with* them—to listen, to learn, and to risk their own standing for the sake of truth told face-to-face. That decision gave rise to the Council on Religion and the Homosexual, one of the earliest sustained efforts by Christian leaders to engage the emerging gay rights movement with theological seriousness and moral humility.

The council was formally organized in 1964 by a coalition of clergy, several of whom were Methodist, including the Reverend Cecil Williams and the Reverend Ted McIlvenna. Their initial posture was not advocacy in the modern political sense but pastoral encounter. These ministers recognized that Christianity—often through silence as much as through condemnation—had inflicted deep harm on gay and lesbian persons. They believed the church could not speak truthfully about human dignity without first hearing the testimony of those it had wounded. Truth, they insisted, must be spoken with wisdom, and wisdom begins with listening.[6]

To that end, Methodist preachers did something that shocked many of their colleagues: They went where gay people actually gathered. Clergy visited gay bars and clubs, not as moral inspectors but as guests. They introduced themselves openly as ministers, asked questions, and listened as patrons described police harassment, family rejection, employment discrimination, and the spiritual trauma inflicted by churches that named them sinful without ever knowing them. These encounters dismantled abstractions. "Homosexuality" ceased to be an idea and became a collection of human lives—beloved by God, shaped by fear and courage, longing for community.

This listening posture soon demanded public courage. On New Year's Eve 1964, the council agreed to cosponsor a fundraising ball for gay organizations at California Hall in San Francisco. What was intended as a festive, dignified event became a flashpoint. Police harassed attendees, photographed guests, and ultimately arrested several clergy who attempted to shield the event and protest the intimidation. The arrests—now remembered as the New Year's Eve Ball arrests—were widely reported in the press. For the first time, many Americans saw Christian ministers being handcuffed not for condemning homosexuals but for standing alongside them.

The significance of that moment cannot be overstated. The clergy did not claim moral perfection or theological finality. Instead, they modeled conviction held with humanity. They believed Christianity had something truthful to say about human relationships and holiness—but they also believed that truth spoken without love becomes a lie. Their courage was not combative; it was relational. It was shaped by love that risked misunderstanding, scandal, and institutional reprisal for the sake of neighbor.

CHAPTER 7
Paul's Witness in Athens, Part 2
Curious Labor (Acts 16:11-15; 17:16-34)

Mike Baughman

The Average Dallasite

"What do you mean, 'the average Dallasite'?"

After several high-profile incidents of racial injustice in our area, we scrapped our worship series plans, rolled up our sleeves, and decided to tackle racial inequity. Our church was packed, frequently to the point of standing room only, for special events and worship services. After introducing a Black community leader who worked at the forefront of racial equity, I listened to his insightful perspective. I kicked off a Q&A

by asking, "What do you most want the average Dallasite to know about race in this city?"

"What do you mean, 'the average Dallasite'?" He tilted his head and looked disappointed, asking a second time because he knew exactly what I meant. I had really meant the average *White* Dallasite, but less than 30 percent of the Dallas population is non-Hispanic White. It is far too easy to assume that "White" or "wealthy" or "Christian" is "normal" or "average," even when data tell us otherwise. My assumption that "average Dallasite" meant "White Dallasite" reveals why cross-cultural ministry is so difficult and so necessary.

Cross-cultural ministry requires wonder, curiosity, humility, and homework to effectively cultivate new life for the church and our community. We have to shed our assumptions about cultural and religious norms. Fortunately, there is a long history and theological tradition at our disposal to help. When planting multiple new congregations, I consistently found myself turning to Paul's examples of cross-cultural ministry, especially in Acts 16:11-15 and 17:16-34. Side by side, these stories bear witness to what does and does not work—what is faithful and what falls short. It may be helpful to read those verses now and keep your Bible handy as we progress through this chapter.

Dogmatic Dissonance

Paul arrives in Athens, is greatly distressed by an abundance of idols, and makes sure to tell everyone about it. Paul latches on to what God would dislike, blustering about idolatry in the synagogue and marketplace. Unlike so many other stories about Paul's ministry, there is no response from the multitudes who follow him. Even the Jews, whom Paul might naturally assume would be upset by idolatry, seem to shrug him off. When one considers the human element in this story, Paul's lack of success makes sense. In a multicultural, densely packed city, people live on top of and around one another. Their day-to-day lives rely upon one another. Hannah, the God-fearing Jewish woman, may live next door to Judah the idol-maker. When Hannah hears Paul lambast idols, she may remember that it was Judah who gave meals to Hannah's family when they were sick or that it was Nicolaus the idolater who gave medicine to Hannah's mother. My guess is that the people in the synagogue had significant conflicting evidence with Paul's general disdain for anyone worshipping idols. Rather than initially wondering what God was up to in Athens, Paul focuses on what God would dislike.

Paul's initial experience in Athens mirrors a pattern I've seen repeatedly. I was raised in a denomination that told me homosexuals were immoral people. Few things dismantled my (mis)understanding of LGBTQ+ persons more than spending time in the musical theater world. A whim audition led to a role as Herod in *Jesus Christ Superstar.* I encountered gay people who were more compassionate, loving, empathetic, community-minded, and full of integrity than most Christians I knew. A queer, agnostic director (himself a college student) taught me lessons about biblical characters and discipleship that still inform my personal faith and practice of ministry today. These experiences introduced a cognitive dissonance that eventually led to a wholesale reevaluation of what I had been taught about theology and biblical interpretation. When doctrine and dogma dismiss human experience, our theology rings hollow. This dissonance seems most common when our theology is formed in cultural isolation, where it becomes all too easy to confuse who Christ is and what culture is. It is far too easy to baptize our assumptions and call them theology or sanctify our comfort zones when Jesus is on the road to Damascus.

Omnipresent Possibilities

Fortunately for Paul, there were others who could see past Paul's bluster. Some of the least likely Athenians—Gentile, secular philosophers—initially write Paul off as "babbling" (see Acts 17:18, NRSVue). Eventually, curiosity leads them to invite him to try sharing his ideas again. Philosophers in Athens are the ones who led Paul to effective cross-cultural ministry! *Paul follows their lead,* trusts their local wisdom, and follows them to the Areopagus. Only after demonstrating his willingness to follow the lead of locals without the benefit of religious privilege does he find success in Athens.

Our church systems are not designed to cultivate cultural and religious humility or curiosity, yet there are theological correctives available to us in our rich heritage. Consider the name of the degree that most clergy attain—a master of divinity—*as if clergy have somehow mastered the divine.* Is there a more pretentious degree than that? It makes sense that pastors would have a spiritual disconnect with people in their communities. We clergy think, rightly so, that our relationship with God is the most important thing in our lives. Our master of divinity degrees and biblical scholarship trick us into thinking that we have superior access to the divine, but God will not be constrained by our institutional accreditation. This omnipresence of God has a rich theological tradition in Catholic natural law, Eastern Orthodox spiritual practices, pilgrimage practices, and Wesley's sermons, to name a few.

When planting congregations and launching new ministries, I've learned to embrace a fundamental principle rooted in the omnipresence of God: When you look for God in others, they tend to see God in you. This is sometimes difficult. John Wesley acknowledges as much in his sermon "On the Omnipresence of God": "What use should we make of this awful consideration [that God is present in all things, places, people]?...Should we not labour continually to acknowledge his presence?"[1] Nonetheless, when we look for God in the people, communities, and cultures we encounter, it levels the religious playing field and softens power dynamics. If I believe that God is at work in all people, then all people (including those who do not go to church) have something to teach me about God. Churches do not exist to bring God into the neighborhood—God is already at work in the neighborhood. Our job is to discover what God is doing in the lives of the people around us and cultivate that Holy Spirit work with wonder, earnest love, and joy.

Mutual Wonder

Paul finds success in Athens when he sheds the privilege afforded by his fancy-pants degrees and curiously takes a wonder-filled approach. Given another chance by Athenian philosophers, he radically shifts his tone:

> *"People of Athens, I see that you are very religious in every way. As I was walking through town and carefully observing your objects of worship, I even found an altar with this inscription: 'To an unknown God.' What you worship as unknown, I now proclaim to you."*
>
> *(Acts 17:22-23)*

He does not call out their idolatry. He celebrates their *religious* tendencies. Rather than call out ignorance, he celebrates their altar to an unknown God and leverages the curiosity inherent in such an altar. Throughout his sermon, he stands side by side with the Athenians in wonder, dropping quotes to popular Stoic and Epicurean philosophy—an ancient equivalent to the way Martin Luther King Jr. quoted the Declaration of Independence in his public speeches or contemporary preachers might quote Beyoncé lyrics in sermons.

His curiosity reveals shared places of wonder and truth between the cultural-religious context from which he comes and the one in which he is in ministry. Though some ridicule Paul, others express interest in continuing the conversation, and others yet "joined him and came to believe" (Acts 17:34).

Curious Labor

When I led a successful church plant with congregants a full generation younger than me, some colleagues called me "the millennial whisperer." It never felt like a compliment. I think it bothered me because it felt dismissive of the labor it took to serve in cross-cultural ministry. I was not chasing some natural instinct. I had to learn enough about the cultures I encountered to grow an appreciation for what mattered to them. Only after that continual, authentic exploration could I align our church's ministry and messaging to the overlapping Venn diagram of Methodist and millennial concerns. This was a repeated process as we engaged new neighborhoods and demographics. To be certain, I botched a lot along the way and would not be described as "cool" by anyone in my church, but people saw me doing the work to find shared spaces of wonder. I was filled with awe at the way God worked through the people I had the chance to serve. They saw me see God in them and asked me about the God who transformed me.

Curiosity alone is not enough for Paul to find success in Athens. Cross-cultural ministry demands immersion. If Paul had not spent time wandering around Athens, immersing himself in the culture, he would not have discovered this altar "to an unknown god" (Acts 17:23). If Paul hadn't spent time listening to Stoic and Epicurean philosophers, he would not have understood what they meant by phrases like "in him we live and move and have our being" (Acts 17:28, NRSVue) or that they understood it to mean the "offspring of God" (Acts 17:29, KJV).

To effectively engage in cross-cultural ministry, we have to likewise spend time in a culture different from our own and listen deeply to the people with whom we would be in ministry.

At the time this book is coming together, a sixty-two-year-old White Texan named Kent Burris is going viral on social media for visiting restaurants where he is a self-described "fish out of water." He owns his ignorance about the food served and the culture of those who serve it. He approaches every plate with an open mind, sweats his way through spice, and offers an open heart to every restaurant worker he encounters. He's quickly endeared himself to Nigerian, Dominican, Ethiopian, Malay, Lebanese, and more audiences, gaining over five hundred thousand followers in just a few months. "His genuine interest and abandonment of control colors each of his TikTok videos and defines his ethos."[2] This folksy Texan responds to almost every comment left on his videos as if they were all from someone dropping by his front porch. Church leaders can follow his lead in our curious labor. We may visit restaurants or coffee shops, parks or soccer leagues, city hall chambers or street protests, Dungeons & Dragons games or gay bars. All of them afford the opportunity for authentic engagement that comes only when we shed our assumption of cultural or religious normativity.

Shedding privilege is not the same as shedding self. While Burris engages culture authentically, he is not a cultural chameleon. He does not shed his Texas lilt, nor does he pretend to fit in. He doesn't seem to stress about always saying the right thing, preferring to lean into the honest thing. Paul, too, finds ways to be authentically himself and express his mission. He engages the opportunity Athenian culture offers him by discussing the nature of the unknown God to which Athenians dedicated an altar. This is as much an act of love as it is a strategy for cross-cultural ministry. He does not simply compliment the Athenians on their religious inclinations and then walk away.

He preaches the gospel that makes him who he is. Paul engages the authentic perspective of Stoic philosophers and then offers his most authentic self—a self transformed by Christ.

Turning This Chapter Upside Down

To close up this chapter, we turn to the story that takes place before Paul enters Athens, where he first steps into a new country and finds his way to meaningful cross-cultural ministry more quickly than he does in Athens. Paul does not launch his ministry in some grand temple or well-established place of learning. His Macedonian ministry begins outside the city gates of Philippi—away from traditional places and people of power. On the Sabbath, he wanders along the riverbank where he "thought there might be a place for prayer" (Acts 16:13). The text describes a gathering of women, using the Greek word commonly used for a religious gathering but with a feminine ending.

Rabbis had educated Paul to believe that a man should not publicly converse with a woman to whom he is not related. Nonetheless, he approaches the women who have gathered outside the city not with authority but with humility. He does not instruct them from a formal standing posture. Instead, he sits, a social demonstration of equality. Though foreign to Paul, Macedonian culture had fewer restrictive norms governing interaction between men and women. Paul steps out of comfort to engage women on a new continent. And it works.

Among the congregation is a powerful woman, Lydia. She runs her own household and a business selling purple cloth to the wealthy. She's a "Gentile God-worshipper" and "the Lord enabled her to embrace Paul's message" (Acts 16:14). She agrees to baptism and takes the lead with a confident touch of irony that is both gracious and assertive, "Now that you have decided that I am a believer in the Lord, come and stay in my house" (Acts 16:15). "Now that you have decided" gets me every time—as if this powerful woman needed Paul's validation of a deep truth she already accepted. Paul relents, is "persuaded" (Acts 16:15), and follows her lead. She takes him in, even though he probably had enough arrogance left in his tone that she would chide him a bit in her invitation.

The stories of Philippi and Areopagus contain lessons for churches that receive pastors from cultures different from those of most of their congregants. I have watched up close as a congregation tried to mold a Black senior pastor into the whitest version they could make him. I know churches that rejected a pastor because they felt uncomfortable with that pastor's generational norms. The early church would have looked far different if Lydia had rejected Paul's accent or if the Athenians had rejected Paul's educational credentials.

As I write this chapter—a modified version of a sermon I've preached many times—I've come to realize that every time I talk about this story, I center on the one with the most power: Paul. But Paul only found success in Philippi and Athens because he found ways to decenter himself. Growth of the early church came as much (if not more) from the open-hearted response of those with whom Paul was in ministry as it did from Paul himself. We credit Paul and put "saint" in front of his name, but the growth of the church and continued ministry in this region occurred only because of Lydia, Dionysius, and Damaris, among others, and the unnamed philosophers who invited Paul to the Areopagus. As we explore the Book of Acts, I hope we—authors and readers—will do a better job than I have of turning our approach upside down to learn as much from the characters around Paul as we learn from him. Just as I had to learn that "average Dallasite" didn't mean what I assumed, we must learn that the margins of biblical stories often hold more wisdom than the center.

Reflection Questions

1. How can you take a page from Burris's example and engage a culture different from yours? This could be generational, racial, economic, or otherwise.

2. Spend time thinking about a culture (other than your own) in which you have been immersed. Draw a big circle on a page and write observations about what you experience in that immersion. Circle the places of shared wonder, joy, interest, truth, or love between what is in that circle and how you might describe your own culture. Is there a starting point in these circled items for meaningful work together?

3. How do you hide your authentic self by engaging people where they are but downplay the significance of Jesus in your life? Do you downplay the significance of your own cultural experiences of food, family, and expectations to fit in?

4. What might you discover in your favorite stories from the Bible by looking at the story not from the perspective of the main character but of the people in the margins of the story?

5. Mike confesses he assumed "average Dallasite" meant "White Dallasite." What assumptions of "normal" or "average" do you carry about your community, workplace, or church? Can you test those assumptions with a look at information available online?

Preaching to the Wyandot

Ashley Boggan

One of my favorite examples of cross-cultural ministry within Methodism is the story of John Stewart. Not the John Stewart of *The Daily Show* fame (sorry, millennials!). This particular John Stewart was a Black man, born free in Virginia in 1786. In his early twenties, he was converted at a Methodist camp meeting. While traveling through Ohio, he felt God's call on his life to go and preach among Indigenous peoples, specifically the Wyandot nation. Stewart was directed to Jonathan Pointer, an African American who, after being captured by the Wyandot, had become fluent in their language. Through Pointer, Stewart preached and sang to the Wyandot. After overcoming some initial resistance, the chiefs and tribal leaders were converted. However, they soon realized that their singing preacher was not officially licensed to preach! Instead of berating and dismissing him, the Wyandot lobbied the Methodist Episcopal Church on Stewart's behalf to grant him a preaching license, which was issued in 1819. With his preaching officially licensed, Stewart was assigned to a mission with the Wyandot.[3] This cross-cultural, immersive ministry led to the founding of the Methodist Missionary Society in 1820 and inspired many others to breach cultural barriers.

CHAPTER 8
When Privilege Runs Out
Paul, the Hissy Fit, and the Long Obedience of Staying (Acts 18; 22; 23)

Aleze Fulbright

Introduction

There is a moment in ministry, and in movements for justice, when confidence curdles into discouragement. It often comes after we have done what we were taught to do: read the books, attend the training sessions, learn the language, listen carefully, and speak thoughtfully. It often comes after we risk public witness and discover that risk does not guarantee affirmation. Instead, we find ourselves more misunderstood, corrected, ridiculed, or dismissed. The applause fades. The resistance hardens. And suddenly the work costs more than we imagined it would.

It is at that moment that privilege reveals itself not as power but as insulation. Privilege can cushion us from the full force of backlash. It can provide exit ramps when the work becomes uncomfortable. It can offer respectable excuses for withdrawal: *I'm tired. I'm not the right person. I don't want to say the wrong thing.* Privilege, in this sense, functions like a temporary shelter. It holds for a while. Then it gives way.

I read Acts with an awareness born of history and lived experience. The option to withdraw from struggle is itself unevenly distributed, because, while tired, I (and those who look like me) never have the option to quit because there are too many looking and far more following in our wake. Additionally, for communities marked by racialized vulnerability, opting out is rarely possible. The systems keep moving. The harm keeps happening. Silence does not stop the wound; it simply hides the bleeding. This chapter makes space for the temptation to retreat from the difficult work of equity while also issuing a clear theological summons to stay. Not because we are perfect. Not because we always get it right. But because faithfulness, in a broken world, often looks like remaining present after privilege has failed.

This chapter attends to what happens when that shelter collapses—essentially, when privilege runs out. It turns to Acts 18:6-10 and Acts 22 and 23 to examine the apostle Paul not at his most heroic but at his most human. This humanity is discouraged, ridiculed, reactive, and tempted to retreat toward easier, safer ministry. Luke's narrative allows us to see Paul throwing what can only be described as a *sanctified hissy fit* (a tantrum). And rather than editing that moment out, Scripture preserves it as revelation.

Discouragement in Corinth

In Acts 18, we encounter a turning point for Paul:

> *When Silas and Timothy arrived from Macedonia, Paul devoted himself to preaching the word and testified to the Jews that Jesus is the Messiah. When they resisted and blasphemed, he shook out his clothes and told them, "Your blood is on your own heads! I am innocent. From now on I will go to the Gentiles."*
>
> *(Acts 18:5-6, CSB)*

Acts 18 opens with Paul arriving in Corinth after a bruising season of ministry. His experience in Athens has not gone as hoped. By the time Paul reaches Corinth, he is financially vulnerable, emotionally depleted, and socially marginal. He takes up work with Aquila and Priscilla not as a strategic choice but as a matter of survival. Tentmaking, here, is not romantic independence; it is economic necessity.

When opposition intensifies, Paul snaps. This is the first glimpse in Acts of a preacher who might want to quit. Paul threatens to retreat, to go where he is welcomed. That instinct is deeply human and prefigures the temptation we feel when the work of justice exhausts us. This is not a carefully discerned missional pivot. It is a reactive declaration born of exhaustion and frustration. Paul is not calmly redirecting strategy; he is lashing out. The symbolic gesture of shaking the dust from his clothes is performative and final. It says, *I'm done. I tried. This is on you.* I find it interesting that Luke does not correct Paul, nor does God immediately intervene with rebuke. Instead, God meets Paul in the aftermath of his outburst. In a vision at night, the Lord says, "Do not be afraid, but speak and do not be silent, for I am with you...for there are many in this city who are my people" (Acts 18:9-10, NRSVue). I believe this passage refutes two distortions: (1) privilege as entitlement (Paul is not entitled to a receptive audience) and (2) privilege as insulation from resistance (discipleship does not promise applause).

What God addresses is not Paul's theology but his fear. Beneath the anger is anxiety. Beneath the dismissal is discouragement. God's word does not deny Paul's pain; it reframes his responsibility. Stay. Speak. Therefore, Paul remains in Corinth for eighteen months. The work he wanted to abandon becomes one of his most sustained ministries. Discouragement was real, but it was not decisive.

We are reminded to trust that the story is larger than our moment of failure. In equity work, whether in the early church, abolition movements, civil rights struggles, or denominational reform, pushback should not be mistaken for failure.

Holy Frustration and Honest Faith

Paul's hissy fit is not an embarrassment to the gospel; it is part of it. Scripture refuses to present faithfulness as emotional stoicism. From the psalms of lament to the weeping of Jeremiah, the Bible insists that frustration, grief, and even anger can coexist with obedience.

In my African American religious tradition, this truth has long been understood. The spirituals were not polite prayers; they were coded cries of anguish and hope. Historically, Black preaching has never required sanitized emotion. It has welcomed tears, raised voices, and trembling hands as signs of a faith that takes suffering seriously. I was taken back to this understanding after the events of the public lynching of George Floyd in May 2020. So many emotions arose because another unarmed Black person died at the hands of law enforcement, and it was only witnessed widely because of the published video. In a virtual meeting with other clergy, trying to gather the words of hope, yet again, a colleague stated, "It is time to return to our roots. It is time for us to lament!" We had experienced the many "thoughts and prayers," which were becoming wearisome to pray. But the word *lament* resonated with many of us as a means of placing the anger, frustration, grief, and sorrow into a process toward healing rather than hiding it or holding our breath for the next occurrence.

Similarly, Paul's outburst belongs in this tradition of holy frustration. It tells the truth about the cost of sustained resistance. It names the emotional labor demanded of those who are continually misunderstood, especially by people who believe they should know better. The problem is not that Paul is frustrated. The danger lies in allowing frustration to justify withdrawal.

God does not shame Paul for being fed up. But God does not release him from responsibility either. The call is not to feel better but to remain faithful.

When Privilege Protects—and Fails

Acts 22 and 23 shift the frame from emotional discouragement to political vulnerability. Paul invokes his Roman citizenship to avoid an illegal flogging. This moment is often celebrated as savvy self-advocacy, and rightly so. Citizenship matters. Rights matter. Privilege, when available, can and should be used to prevent unnecessary harm. Yet Luke is careful not to portray privilege as salvific. Here, Paul's privilege has run out because his Roman citizenship does not spare him from being bound. His reputation does not protect him from mob violence. His theological acumen does not calm the crowd. Paul's appeal escalates rather than resolves the conflict. His speech before the council descends into chaos. A plot emerges to assassinate him. He is transferred under heavy military guard, not as a respected leader but as a dangerous liability.

In Acts 22 and 23, Paul experiences what many of us know too well: The ground beneath you gives way, and the things that once sustained you no longer do. Paul is forced to speak into confusion, defend himself against slander, and grapple with his own fear. Paul's citizenship saves his body but not his peace. It buys him time, not freedom. It protects him temporarily, not permanently. Privilege delays suffering; it does not erase it. For people who are engaged in racial equity work, this distinction is critical. Institutional standing, education, or social capital may shield leaders for a season. But when the work threatens entrenched power, protection wears thin. When resistance comes, it is often a sign that one is touching entrenched power. When privilege runs out, only calling remains.

Racism, Correction, and the Desire to Exit

Paul's experience in Acts 18, 22, and 23 is not an isolated ancient story. It is the pattern of those who pursue justice beyond comfort. In contemporary conversations about racism, many leaders, particularly those with relative privilege, experience a predictable cycle. There is enthusiasm, followed by resistance; learning, followed by missteps; correction, followed by defensiveness or shame. And then comes the temptation to withdraw: *It does not seem to be changing the system, so I should stop trying.* From the perspective of marginalized communities, this withdrawal feels less like humility and more like abandonment. It places the emotional comfort of the privileged above the survival needs of the vulnerable. As theologian James H. Cone argued, racism persists not only through overt hatred but through the quiet withdrawal of those who could have stood firm.[1]

History bears witness to leaders who faced Paul's temptation and chose to stay. The witness of Frederick Douglass comes to mind. Douglass grew increasingly disillusioned with White abolitionists who applauded his testimony while resisting his authority. He was corrected, constrained, and often silenced. Withdrawal would have been understandable. Instead, Douglass deepened his critique, insisting that freedom required confronting racism within reform movements themselves.[2] Or consider Fannie Lou Hamer, a sharecropper and civil rights activist, who endured violence, poverty, and ridicule. Her exhaustion was real, but it did not lead to disengagement. "I'm sick and tired of being sick and tired," she declared, not as resignation, but as resolve.[3] Her courage took her into jails, fields of voter suppression, and spaces of brutal resistance. Hamer had little economic privilege, but her moral authority reshaped national consciousness. She knew that, without privilege or safety nets, retreating was not an option. Her fatigue became fuel. And, contextually, Black clergy serve in predominantly White institutions. We see this across American church history, where Black clergy have labored within institutions slow to repent. Many experienced Paul's frustration with the strong desire to shake the dust and walk away. Some did. Others stayed, pressing for transformation at great personal cost. Their witnesses remind us that institutional change is often purchased with endurance.

Acts challenges the church to rethink privilege. Privilege is not sin in itself. Paul uses his. The issue is not possession but posture. Privilege becomes spiritually dangerous when it is used as permission to disengage from costly obedience.

Paul's story refuses to sanctify exit strategies. Even when corrected, even when endangered, even when disillusioned, Paul does not abandon witness. His methods evolve. His locations change. But the work continues. Those without privilege do not have the option to disengage from racism. The gospel calls those with relative power to match their endurance to the endurance of the oppressed, not as saviors but as companions.

A Pastoral Word to the Weary

To those tempted to retreat: Scripture makes room for our frustration. God hears it. God honors our honesty. But God also says, "Do not be afraid, but speak and do not be silent" (Acts 18:9, NRSVue). Do not be afraid. Do not be silent. Stay. When privilege runs out, presence remains. Obedience remains. Hope remains—not hope in success but hope in the God who meets us in the night and calls us forward.

At the heart of this chapter is an incarnational claim. In Jesus Christ, God does not withdraw from human suffering when misunderstood or rejected. God stays. God absorbs conflict. God remains present even unto death.

When privilege runs out, the gospel's true demand becomes visible. There is no recourse to safety that exempts disciples from solidarity with the vulnerable. Paul's call to remain in Corinth echoes this divine pattern. The work of equity is not an accessory to the gospel; it is participation in God's staying power. It is slow, costly, and often invisible. But it is the shape of faithfulness.

Conclusion

Privilege is helpful; its loss is not fatal. The gospel does not promise ease, escape, or applause. I believe it promises presence—God's presence. Paul's story is not one of unbroken courage. It is a testimony to perseverance after ease evaporates. The church today stands at a similar threshold. The work of equity is demanding, humbling, and often thankless. The temptation to withdraw is real.

Acts insists that God's purposes unfold through those who stay, who learn from correction, who endure misunderstanding, and who refuse to abandon the struggle simply because it costs them.

When privilege runs out, faith begins again. Additionally, this chapter argues that when privilege runs out, real discipleship begins and then deepens. It explores how Paul's breakdowns become breakthroughs, how failures refine prophetic voices, and how those historically marginalized and without privilege have no option but to stay in the struggle and rewrite the narrative of justice.

Reflection Questions

1. Paul wanted to quit ministry in Corinth after facing ridicule and resistance. Mike owns this instinct in chapter 2. Aleze has found herself tired so many times. When have you been tempted to withdraw from equity work because it became uncomfortable, you became too tired, or you felt like you were not being effective? What kept you engaged, or what caused you to step away?

2. Aleze observes, "Privilege can cushion us from the full force of backlash. It can provide exit ramps when the work becomes uncomfortable." Do you benefit from "exit ramps"? If so, have you taken advantage of them in the past?

3. When have you observed privilege "running out" in yourself or others?

4. Unpack Aleze's statement, "When privilege runs out, faith begins again." How does that align or not align with your experiences?

We Hoped to Change Things: It Only Took Twenty Years

Ashley Boggan

For decades within The United Methodist Church, LGBTQ+ clergy and laity lived under a paradox that cut to the heart of vocation. They were baptized, educated, examined, and called. Many were affirmed by congregations and bore visible fruit in ministry. Yet because of their sexual orientation or their willingness to live openly, they were denied ordination, prohibited from celebrating marriages, and—when conscience required honesty—subjected to church trials and the loss of credentials. What is striking is not only that some resisted these exclusions but that many chose to remain. They stayed as witnesses, practicing what might be called costly obedience.

Among the most emblematic of these figures is Beth Stroud. Ordained an elder in the East Pennsylvania Conference, Stroud was a gifted pastor and theologian, serving congregations with care and intellectual rigor. Early in the first decade of the twenty-first century, when denominational law explicitly prohibited "self-avowed practicing homosexuals" from ordination, Stroud made the decision to live honestly about who she was.[4] That decision did not come cheaply. In 2004, after a highly publicized church trial, she was found guilty under church law and stripped of her ministerial credentials.[5]

Defrocking is not only a professional loss; it is a spiritual wounding. It tells a person that the church to which they have given their life no longer recognizes their call. For many, that moment would have been an understandable exit point. Stroud had every reason—emotionally, vocationally, and theologically—to disengage. Instead, she stayed.

After her trial, Beth Stroud remained United Methodist. She worshipped in a local United Methodist congregation. She continued to live within the rhythms of a church that had publicly declared her unfit for ordained ministry. She did not stay because it was comfortable. She stayed because she understood staying itself as a form of witness. Her presence in the pews—no longer behind the pulpit—was a quiet but powerful refusal to allow exclusion to have the final word.[6]

Stroud was not alone in this posture. Earlier figures such as Jimmy Creech, who was defrocked in the late 1990s for officiating at same-gender unions, also chose to remain connected to the church, even when their ministry took forms outside traditional appointment structures.[7] And there are countless named and unnamed LGBTQ+ siblings in Christ who either remained closeted, left the denomination, or stayed whose ministries and faith deserve affirmation. These leaders did not confuse institutional loyalty with naivete. They knew precisely what the church was doing. Yet they believed that the gospel demanded presence, not disappearance; testimony, not retreat.

What distinguished Stroud's staying was its theological clarity. She did not remain because she lacked alternatives, nor because she believed suffering itself was virtuous. She stayed because she recognized a greater danger: that privilege—when used as permission to disengage from costly obedience—can hollow out faith. For those with education, mobility, and other ecclesial or social privileges, leaving an unjust system can be framed as a matter of moral clarity. But for Stroud, obedience meant remaining in tension, trusting that God's work in the church would not be accomplished only by those in power.

That trust was vindicated, though not quickly. In 2024, when the General Conference of The United Methodist Church removed the discriminatory language that had barred LGBTQ+ persons from ordination and marriage, the moment carried particular weight for those who had paid its cost. Stroud was among the first to receive her credentials back—an act not of charity but of restoration. The church did not "give" her a calling; it finally acknowledged the one it had long denied.

Her reinstatement did not erase the years of loss, nor did it retroactively justify the harm done. But it testified to something deeper—that staying can itself be a sacrament of hope. In an article detailing her first time blessing the sacrament of Communion after her credentials were restored, Stroud stated, "We hoped my coming out would change things. And it did. It was one piece of a larger movement; but it did change things. Here we are.... It only took 20 years."[8] Stroud's story reminds the church that obedience is not measured by comfort or speed but by faithfulness under pressure. Privilege becomes spiritually dangerous when it allows us to leave before love has finished its work. Stroud stayed, not because it was easy, but because she believed the church was worth the cost—and because the gospel, as she understood it, demanded nothing less.

CHAPTER 9

A Time to Keep Silent

(Acts 19:23-41; 20:7-12)

Mike Baughman

Theological Packing Peanuts

"Why did you keep talking?" the veteran chaplain asked me. We were going over a verbatim account of a visit I had that week with a dying patient. I was new to chaplaincy, ministry, and the uncomfortable realities of hospitals.

"What do you mean?" I asked. I had expected nothing but praise from the room of chaplains for my thoughtful and brilliant theological articulation. After repeated critique sessions of "constructive criticism," I thought I had finally done something right and praiseworthy in a foreign world by leaning on one of my strongest gifts—teaching.

"Why did you keep talking here," she pointed to the page, "for paragraphs!" Her eyes went a little wide.

"I thought the patient was struggling to understand God, and I thought I had a good way to explain." A defensive edge grew in my voice.

"But she didn't ask about God. In fact, she seemed silent for a long time. Were there silent gaps between things you said?"

I told my supervisor, "No," even though I realized there had been a lot of silence in the conversation. I had packed the conversation gaps with theological packing peanuts meant to soften the edge of silence in the face of death.

"Looking at what little she said, I don't think your patient asked for any of this. What if you had just sat with her while she was dying? I wonder if she was more comfortable with her death than you were."

Before that hospital reflection moment, very little in my life had trained me to refrain from speaking. College, seminary, family, church gigs, and volunteer opportunities had always celebrated my ability to speak. I was rewarded with good grades, favorable reviews, and plenty of positive attention. While I have become much better at learning when to be quiet in moments of pastoral care, it's taken me decades to develop an instinct for discerning when to speak and when to keep silent.

St. Paul of Verbose City

The Scriptures paint a clear picture of Paul as someone who is unafraid to open his mouth and share his thoughts. In the lead-up to the stories we explore in this chapter, Paul is full of big preacher energy. Pentecost has just repeated itself—but this time in Ephesus and under Paul's leadership instead of Peter's (Acts 19:1-7). Bolstered by such success, "Paul went to the synagogue and *spoke confidently for the next three months*" (Acts 19:8a, emphasis added). He offers "convincing arguments concerning the nature of God's kingdom" (Acts 19:8b), which leads to miracles, empowered disciples, lives changed, repentance offered, value systems changed, inequities addressed, and people running around naked because even evil spirits know who Paul is (Acts 19:8b-20). Admittedly, that last outcome seems weird, but the rest had to be pretty confidence-building for Paul and his preaching.

Transformative faith, rightly lived, inevitably disrupts systems because faithful living pushes against cultural norms of comfort in its effort to cultivate a more perfect union of God, city, and culture. Of the societal systems disrupted, few are more upsetting to the powers that be (translation: people who benefit from existing systems) than economic disruption. The success of the early Ephesian church disrupted an economy built around idolatry, tourism, and the Temple to Artemis. Wealthy silversmiths who benefited from "an easy living" (Acts 19:25) positioned Paul and the Ephesian church as a threat to the economic, cultural, and religious viability not only of Ephesus but also "the entire civilized world" (Acts 19:27). To this day, we see wealthy self-interest stir up crowds with rhetoric full of hyperbole and empty of truth. These outlooks fail to see the potential for new, more righteous systems. Ephesus was thrown into turmoil, craftsmen were threatening to riot, and an assembly at the city theater was called, where a silent miracle prevented disaster: "Paul wanted to appear before the assembly, but the disciples wouldn't allow him" (Acts 19:30).

For the first time in three months, Paul was quiet. Because he listened to local disciples and kept his mouth shut, angry voices no longer had the lightning rod of an articulated Pauline position. Their energy started to dissipate. Of all people, the Artemis-worshipping city manager calmed the crowd and spared the early Ephesian church from persecution. From that point forward, Paul never preached in Ephesus again. He spoke only with Ephesian church leaders, trusting them to lead the church forward. And it thrived.

Training Ourselves

While working for equity, those of us with privilege ought to attend to Paul's example. Sometimes the most powerful thing we can do is step back and let others lead. Learning to keep silent does not always come naturally. There are surely times when it has been important for me to speak up for those who are marginalized. I sometimes have access to rooms full of White faces or heterosexual-identifying persons. Sometimes, women who are understandably fatigued from facing constant waves of patriarchy are relieved that a man can articulate a feminist ideal or name a patriarchal assumption. White folks created white supremacy, and men have cultivated patriarchy—White men surely have a role in dismantling those systems. Sometimes that role is to step away from the microphone.

When people with privilege speak too often, take up too much airtime, or make too many decisions, they can undermine a movement toward equity *even when saying all the right things*. There are far too many times that I've embodied supremacy in my effort to dismantle it simply because I assumed I could or should work alone or prioritize my leadership instead of my capacity to support the leadership of others.

I am a part of The United Methodist Church, where we love methodology and order so much that church legislation is sometimes a spiritual discipline (I say that while adjusting my church nerd glasses). Several years ago, my annual conference (most denominations have a general equivalent of a regional body like a diocese, presbytery, or synod) identified itself as more progressive. This clear cultural definition not only made a way for greater inclusion among LGBTQ+ persons in our area but also likely reduced the number of churches that would ultimately disaffiliate in later years. Despite those outcomes, our initial efforts were not generally received favorably by people in power. One of our most successful moments came when I consulted with closeted and openly gay United Methodists, as well as allies, to draft legislation that moved our conference toward greater equity. We decided, though, that I would not formally present or propose the legislation. Other leaders—whose support for LGBTQ+ inclusion was less publicly known and therefore less likely to trigger automatic opposition—prominently signed and presented words that I had largely strung together. Our efforts would have been far less successful if I had stood at a podium and made the presentation. Looking back on these pivotal decisions, I'm reminded of Paul's silence in the Ephesus town hall.

In contrast, there have been other times that I stepped in to present public arguments for racial or gender equity and was far less collaborative with persons of color or female-identifying leadership. These efforts failed. When privileged people prioritize their own voices, they unwittingly create stumbling blocks for those already leading from the margins. Fortunately, colleagues saw my good intentions and later invited me to walk alongside them. This was an act of grace—one I am not entitled to receive for my intentions alone. They trusted me enough to show me the problems I accidentally created. I'm learning to listen.

I've tried to consistently use the language of "co-conspiracy" for this very reason. Self-conspiracies are generally delusional. Co-conspiracies are divine—after all, Jesus said he is with us when "two or three gather" in his name (see Matthew 18:20). Christian world-changing is not a solo mission. One cannot launch a self-conspiracy and expect those who have been marginalized to jump on their bandwagon. To believe otherwise is another form of white supremacy and patriarchy.

Practically Cultivating Quiet

I want to get super practical on how to get better at this—knowing when to speak and when to step away from a microphone, so to speak.

Silence is tricky—it can be a tool of oppression that allows oppression to continue unquestioned, but it can also be an act of resistance. The difference is made by whose voice is amplified by your silence. Complicit silence allows harm to continue. Strategic silence holds space for new leaders. A few practices have been helpful to me: counting, deferring, and naming.

Counting

Counting is as simple and straightforward as it sounds: Literally track who is speaking and how often. From 2014 to 2017, I routinely served on panels put together by the LGBTQ+ and Women's Center at a nearby university. Most members of the panel identified as queer. It was helpful, their director said, to articulate a more inclusive theology when people ask religious questions so that queer panelists don't have to bear as much of the brunt of religious trauma from their past. After the first two panels, the director thanked me for attending but pointed out how much I spoke.

"Really?" I asked, surprised because I hadn't noticed it—not because I didn't believe them.

"Yeah. I mean, you aren't talking any more than any other panelist, but the panel is more about them, so maybe you can chime in a little less."

"Heard," I responded, and they scheduled me for another panel. I started keeping tally marks in future panels. If my tally or the collective heterosexual tally was too high, I'd refrain from chiming in on a group question or ask whether other panelists had thoughts before answering questions directed at me. Since that time, I've carried this practice into staff and board meetings, Bible studies, and more. If I am committed to elevating other voices, I need to make space for other voices to speak. It's hard to argue with my own tally mark data when they're staring me in the face. It's made me choosier about what I share, which I believe has the added benefit of making my statements more meaningful when I do choose to speak. To some readers, this might sound so basic, but the world does not train people with privilege to temper their voices. We must take it upon ourselves to train ourselves.

Deferring

The people most affected by decisions should have a say in making those decisions. This is the fundamental principle behind so many of our notions of fairness, democracy, and representational government. Ideally, the board of directors of a nonprofit exists to defend the interests of those for whom it exists and should have representatives from that community. Deferring my privilege means incorporating multiple stakeholders into decision-making, trusting that others see things I do not. Paul, an established and undeniably effective leader, trusted the wisdom of the Ephesian leaders who told him to remain quiet when he wanted nothing more than to speak. Paul's witness demonstrates again and again that equitable leadership requires trusting others.

When I am unsure whether it is best to speak up and leverage my privilege or to be quiet and make space for others, I sometimes check in with a trusted friend or the entire room. I might awkwardly say, "I'm not sure if this is a time where I should speak up or not, but I'm uncomfortable with something that just took place." Sometimes naming the awkward realities is the right choice when I'm not sure what to say.

Deferring the microphone can be uncomfortable for leaders who are used to speaking on behalf of their church or community. A guilty pleasure of mine is watching White church leaders the first few times they show up at events led by Black community leaders. I swear I can see them physically tense when they first hear Black leaders quote Malcolm X, make reference to thug life, speak well of the Black Panthers, or cite Martin Luther King Jr.'s perspective on anything but his most easily agreeable statements that flood Facebook every January. I was that pastor until I started listening to a broad range of King's sermons, researching Tupac, and familiarizing myself with the enormous good the Black Panthers did, despite what I was taught in US history class. Deferring the microphone has taught me a great deal about what I have to learn.

Noticing and Naming

After listening to enough women discuss the phenomenon, I began to notice men—including myself—interrupt women *all the time*. In addition to retraining myself to wait before speaking, I've made it my annoying habit to interrupt interrupters and say something like, "Hold on one second, I'm not sure Carly was done with that thought, and I'm curious about it. Carly, was there more?" I find that moments like these simultaneously leverage my power by interrupting someone else with privilege and divest my power by immediately turning the microphone over to someone who had the microphone stolen from them.

Noticing and naming go beyond interrupting speakers. When consulting with nonprofit boards, I've noticed and named when leadership is all White for a church or nonprofit that claims to be in service to a population that is entirely made up of persons of color. I've noticed and named to large funding agencies that no one in their grant decision-making is, or has ever been, a part of a nonprofit organization. I try to apply this practice to myself—noticing and naming when I fall short or contribute imperfectly to a conversation that calls for more. That includes this book. We are limited by our own experience. It is only a partial offering, which can and must be supplemented by other stories, wisdom, communities, and context if we are to be a worldwide church. I look forward to conversations about what we missed, got wrong, or could have improved to cultivate a more fruitful dialogue.

A Cautionary Tale and Opportunity Missed

Paul does not always know when to stay silent. If I were the pope and could fast-track sainthood, I'd do it for Eutychus and name him the patron saint of those who are bored in church. One of the funniest cautionary tales in the Bible comes to us in Acts 20:7-12. With only one day left before heading on to a brief stop in Ephesus, Paul takes it upon himself in Troas to say out loud every thought he has ever had. As best as biblical scholars can tell, the *first part* of his sermon went six to seven hours. A young man—we'll call him "Saint Eutychus"—found Paul's sermon so inspirational that he fell, quite literally, dead asleep "as Paul talked on and on. When he was sound asleep, he fell from the third floor and died" (Acts 20:9). Yikes.

Paul rushes downstairs, out the door, *raises Eutychus from the dead*, goes right back upstairs, and fails to read the room. You'd think he'd take that incident as a cue to wrap it up and send everyone home. Instead, Paul "talked for a long time—right up until daybreak" (Acts 20:11). Unlike so many of Paul's other preaching stories, this text does not name anyone coming to faith, being baptized, understanding the gospel, or experiencing any positive outcomes whatsoever, apart from the fact that they "took the young man away alive, and they were greatly comforted" (Acts 20:12). Something tells me the church in Troas wasn't about to headline a big event with St. Paul of Verbose City!

On the one hand, I don't know what to do with this story. Resurrection is a stunningly rare miracle in the Bible. Paul never resurrects someone who dies from violence or disease. His only resurrection miracle is reserved for someone he bored to death! On the other hand, I see in this story a reminder that even though Paul learned to hold his tongue in Ephesus, knowing when to be silent isn't a one-and-done lesson. I suspect that knowing when to speak and when to refrain from speaking requires lifelong discipline.

Letting Silence Pray

In my third and final year as a hospital chaplain, I was working a late-night shift at a hospital, standing next to Hank, an ICU patient who was dying. I had spent time with him days before. He'd been responsive. He was the type of patient who muttered "Yes, Jesus" and "Please, Lord" when I prayed. Some patients rely on a chaplain to speak to God on their behalf, but not Hank. His prayers were longer than mine and full of praise. He was the kind of person you knew briefly but suspected you could have been friends with if only there had been more time.

At 1:30 a.m., I crawled my way through the dark hospital room's spiderweb of tubes and cords to visit with Hank. His breath was all that was left of him. He would not hear my words, nor would he speak any in response. I began to leave and then stopped. Hank had faithfully dedicated his whole life to God. In these final moments, the only thing he had left was his breath. So I joined with him in the prayer he had already started, speaking as he inhaled and pausing as he exhaled. "God," Hank exhaled. "I'm sitting next to your servant Hank." He exhaled again. "He has dedicated his life to you." He exhaled again. "And so now he dedicates his breath." Hank exhaled. "Until he has nothing left to give." Hank exhaled. "And then will dedicate his death." Hank exhaled. "Receive now his final gifts." Hank exhaled. I then sat in silence while Hank prayed because I knew his offering was far more important than any words I could assemble.

When do we speak for those who will be ignored? When do we keep silent to reduce the noise and thereby make quieter voices heard?

These are tricky questions that demand attention, care, and a lifetime of learning. I am glad I stayed in the room with Hank, even though my voice wasn't what mattered. Sometimes the most sacred thing we can offer is our presence without our voice—whether at a deathbed or in a movement for justice. There are lessons in that hospital room as well for those of us who co-conspire with those who have been oppressed.

Reflection Questions

1. How do you personally know when to speak up and when to keep silent?
2. When have you spoken way too long or far too often?
3. Very practically speaking, what can you do in the next week or month to make sure that you are listening to marginalized voices? Is there a way that you can commit to count, defer, or notice and name, or do you have a different idea in mind?
4. When have you experienced the power of a silent presence—whether by offering it or receiving it? How can that experience inform your work for equity?

"Many Would Rather Hear Him Than the Bishops"[1]

Ashley Boggan

Early Methodism, in Wesley's day, was mostly dominated by White male voices—those of John Wesley himself, of his brother and hymnist Charles Wesley, or the ever-eccentric voice of George Whitefield. White women and White laymen did exhort and preach alongside Wesley, but the overall tone of early Methodism was White and male. This carried over into American Methodism. Francis Asbury, soon to be "Bishop Asbury," was traveling long distances throughout the newly formed United States and was in dire need of support. To whom did he turn? A formerly enslaved, illiterate, Black Methodist man named Harry Hosier.[2]

Bishop Asbury records in his journal, "I have thought if I had two horses, and Harry (a coloured man) to go with, and drive one, and meet the black people; and to spend about six months in Virginia and the Carolinas, it would be attended with a blessing."[3]

Soon after, traveling through Virginia in 1781, Asbury's journal records the first instance of a sermon given by a Black man to a Black congregation (with White listeners nearby): "Sunday 13, Preached at the chapel; afterward Harry, a black man, spoke on the barren fig-tree. This circumstance was new, and the white people looked on with attention."[4] Later that year, we can see evidence that Harry's preaching was quite successful, even among predominantly White audiences. Asbury records, "Harry seems to be unwilling to go with me; I fear his speaking so much to White people in the city, has been, or will be, injurious; he has been flattered, and may be ruined."[5] Here, it seems that Harry's preaching has been so popular that Asbury fears that he's being *flattered*. Perhaps this flattery was justified. Martin Boehm, of United Brethren in Christ lineage, said of Harry's preaching, "His voice was musical, and his tongue as the pen of a ready writer. He was unboundedly popular, and many would rather hear him than the bishops."[6]

However, no matter where they traveled, Asbury frequently gave Hosier the pulpit, choosing to set aside his own voice and privilege and highlight the eloquence of a formerly enslaved Black man. Hosier also traveled with other White male preachers such as Freeborn Garrettson, and they, too, often gave him the pulpit. It is believed that Hosier and Bishop Coke traveled over one thousand miles on horseback together.

The journal of Rev. Dr. Thomas Coke (the second bishop of The Methodist Episcopal Church) describes Hosier as one of the most eloquent people he'd ever heard, despite his lack of education. Hosier's preaching style and hermeneutical capabilities were of God, according to Coke: "I think I never heard a man speak better in my life. What learning could not give, God had given him."[7] Hosier traveled some with Coke as well. Coke recorded some of these instances in his journal:

> I have now had the pleasure of hearing Harry preach several times. I sometimes give notice immediately after preaching, that in a little time Harry will preach to the blacks; but the whites always stay to hear him. Sometimes I publish him to preach at candle-light, as the negroes can better attend at that time. I really believe he is one of the best preachers in the world, there is such an amazing power attends his preaching, though he cannot read; and he is one of the humblest creatures I ever saw.[8]

In a similar vein to how Paul handled choosing silence, Bishop Asbury and Bishop Coke often deferred to Harry Hosier, an uneducated, formerly enslaved Black man, because his preaching had proven to be more effective than any other.

CHAPTER 10

Claiming Sacred Citizenship

Asserting Our Rights for the Sake of the Gospel (Acts 22:25-28; 23:12-35)

Aleze Fulbright

Introduction

I was raised in a tradition that taught me how to endure. Endure hardship. Endure misunderstanding. Endure injustice. Endure disappointment from the world, from the church, and sometimes from God's people themselves. I know what it means to love the church and still be harmed by systems, ecclesial and civic, that were never designed with people like me in mind. I know what it means to serve communities whose very existence feels inconvenient to the powers that be. And I know how quickly churches can be pressured into shrinking their witness under the guise of keeping the peace.

For generations, the Christian church, particularly in communities shaped by oppression, has been formed by a theology of endurance. We have been taught how to survive unjust systems even when those systems refuse to recognize our humanity. This enduring faith has often been what sustained us when the law failed us, when the courts denied us, and when the nation betrayed its own promises. Endurance has often been framed as a spiritual virtue and resistance as a moral risk. Somewhere along the way, suffering became synonymous with faithfulness, and silence was baptized as humility. And yet, there is a danger in allowing endurance to become our only theological register. In such a framework, asserting one's rights can feel unfaithful, even antagonistic to the gospel. But Scripture tells a more complicated and honest story.

In Acts 22 and 23, the apostle Paul refuses the false choice between faith and agency. He refuses to confuse submission with silence. And he refuses to allow injustice to masquerade as God's will. Paul survives and, more important, thrives in ministry not only because he is called but because he is informed. He knows his rights and privileges. He asserts them. And in doing so, he safeguards both his body and his mission. Paul demonstrates a form of discipleship that is both spiritually grounded and politically literate. Paul does not abandon faith for law, nor does he substitute citizenship for calling. Instead, he understands that knowing and asserting one's rights can be a faithful strategy for sustaining ministry, protecting life, and advancing the gospel.

This chapter suggests that knowing and asserting our rights as churches, as congregants, and as citizens is not a betrayal of the gospel.

It is, in many cases, a faithful expression of it. At a moment when many churches in the United States and around the world are increasingly scrutinized, restricted, and sometimes criminalized for their ministries with marginalized populations, Paul's witness presses an urgent question upon the contemporary church: What happens when we forget our rights or spiritualize our own dispossession?

Paul, the Prisoner Who Refuses to Be Powerless

Acts 22 situates Paul at the intersection of religious hostility and state violence. He has been falsely accused of defiling the temple, seized by an enraged mob, and delivered into Roman custody. The tribune orders him to be interrogated by flogging, a common Roman practice designed to extract information through pain. Luke describes the scene with chilling brevity: "They stretched him out for the lash" (Acts 22:25, CSB). His body is positioned for punishment before any verdict has been rendered. It is at this precise moment that Paul speaks. "Is it legal for you to flog a Roman person who is uncondemned?" (Acts 22:25, NRSVue). This is not rhetorical flourish. It is a legal challenge. This is not defiance for defiance's sake. It is not arrogance. It is clarity. Paul does not appeal to his apostleship. He does not invoke martyrdom. He invokes the law.

Roman citizenship conferred specific protections, among them the right to due process and immunity from summary punishment. To violate these rights placed Roman officials themselves in jeopardy. Violating them put soldiers and commanders at risk of severe punishment. As soon as Paul names his status, the power dynamics shift. Fear moves up the chain of command. The centurion alerts the powers that be. Those powers confirm Paul's citizenship and withdraw the order immediately. Paul's suffering is interrupted not by a miracle but by knowledge. For communities whose bodies have historically been deemed expendable and historically treated as disposable—such as enslaved Africans, Black women, immigrants, and the poor, to name a few—Paul's refusal resonates deeply. He models a faith that refuses to surrender dignity in the name of devotion. This moment is theologically significant because Paul does not frame the beating as spiritually inevitable. He does not accept unnecessary harm as a badge of honor. He understands that his body is not expendable, even for the gospel. He does not accept injustice as God's will. Nor does he confuse endurance with faithfulness. Instead, he asserts his rights calmly, clearly, and without apology.

Calling Does Not Require the Abdication of Agency

One of the most corrosive lies perpetuated within the church is the notion that obedience requires passivity. Marginalized Christians are often taught that resistance signals a lack of trust in God, while submission, no matter how harmful, is framed as virtue. We are told to pray rather than protest. To forgive rather than confront. To trust God rather than challenge systems. I believe Paul dismantles this theology. Paul is willing to suffer for the gospel, but he is not willing to be abused unnecessarily. He discerns when suffering is redemptive and when it is simply destructive.

This distinction is crucial, especially for churches that serve communities already burdened by systemic violence. Today, churches engaged in ministry with immigrants, unhoused persons, LGBTQ+ youth, and communities of color are facing increasing legal and political pressure. Faith leaders have been investigated for providing humanitarian aid at the southern border. Pastors have been arrested for protesting unjust laws. Congregations offering sanctuary have been surveilled and threatened. Zoning ordinances are used to shut down food pantries. Surveillance is used to intimidate activists. Ministries of mercy are recast as acts of subversion. Ministry is no longer assumed to be protected simply because it is religious. And too often, churches respond by retreating, mistaking quietness for wisdom and caution for faith. As journalist Heidi Schlumpf notes, "What was once understood as an expression of religious conviction is now increasingly framed as criminal activity."[1] The result is a climate of fear that pressures churches to retreat from their prophetic witness. Paul's example challenges this retreat. Faithfulness, he shows us, sometimes requires confrontation rather than withdrawal. Additionally, Paul offers a corrective. He shows us that discernment sometimes looks like resistance.

In Acts 23, the danger escalates. More than forty men conspire to assassinate Paul, binding themselves with an oath to kill him. This is not impulsive violence; it is organized, premeditated, and sanctioned by religious leaders. Yet Paul survives, not through spectacle, but through procedure. When Paul's nephew overhears the plot and reports it, the Roman commander responds decisively, assembling an overwhelming security detail to escort Paul—and not just a security detail but a massive military escort. Two hundred soldiers, seventy cavalry, and two hundred spearmen are mobilized to transport Paul safely to Caesarea. Utilizing legal protections is not a betrayal of faith. It is often the means through which God preserves life and mission. Luke records this in almost bureaucratic detail, underscoring the irony: The same imperial system that threatened Paul now protects him when its own laws are followed. This narrative refuses a simplistic theology that pits God against government in absolute terms. God works here through law, bureaucracy, and state authority, deeply flawed as they may be. This is an example the church needs to be reminded of. Engaging legal systems does not mean affirming them. Utilizing rights does not mean trusting governments more than God. It means recognizing that God often works through imperfect structures to accomplish divine purposes.

Contemporary Victories: When the Church Asserts Its Rights

In the United States, we are witnessing an unsettling pattern. The church is increasingly confronted with the reality that religious freedom is not self-executing; it must be exercised, defended, and asserted. Ministries once assumed to be protected now operate under suspicion.

In 2019, faith leaders who provided food and water to migrants in the Arizona desert faced a federal investigation.[2] In 2020 and 2021, clergy were arrested for protesting voter suppression laws and racial injustice. In multiple cities, churches serving unhoused populations have been targeted through zoning restrictions and nuisance ordinances designed to shut down ministries without directly confronting their religious purpose.[3] Legal scholar Katherine Stewart observes, "Religious liberty is being selectively applied—expanded for some expressions of faith while restricted for others, particularly those that challenge political power."[4] Silence will not save us; neither will naivete.

Paul's witness offers the modern church several enduring lessons: First, legal literacy is a spiritual discipline. Ignorance leaves communities vulnerable. Knowledge empowers faithful action. Second, asserting rights is not faithlessness; it is stewardship. Paul protects his body because it carries the gospel. Third, not all suffering is redemptive. The church must learn to distinguish between sacrificial suffering and preventable harm. Fourth, the law is a tool, not a god. It can be used without being worshipped. And finally, protecting people protects the mission. When bodies are broken unnecessarily, ministries are silenced prematurely.

For Black churches, this moment feels painfully familiar. Historically, whenever the church has aligned itself with liberation, abolition, desegregation, or voting rights, it has been met with surveillance, intimidation, and violence. The present moment is not new; it is recurring. The Black church has never been naive about the relationship between faith and citizenship. From Reconstruction through the civil rights movement, Black pastors preached Scripture alongside constitutional principles. Sanctuaries doubled as civic classrooms. Bible studies included voter education. Sermons named both Pharaoh and the Supreme Court. Paul would recognize this strategy.

This double consciousness, as so eloquently coined by Dr. W. E. B. Du Bois, was not accidental. It was necessary. Historian Evelyn Brooks Higginbotham reminds us, "The Black church functioned as one of the few institutions where spiritual formation and political education could coexist."[5] These actions happened because churches knew their rights and refused to surrender them quietly. I stand within this lineage. My ordination, my education, my vote, and my voice are all fruits of legal struggle as much as spiritual calling. None of these were guaranteed. They were claimed. Paul belongs to this tradition of sacred citizenship.

Conclusion

Paul does not survive Acts 22 and 23 by accident. He survives because he knows who he is, whose he is, and what the law affords him. His courage is not only spiritual; it is informed.

In an era when churches are pressured to shrink their witness, sanitize their compassion, and spiritualize injustice, they risk unnecessary martyrdom and preventable loss. Paul reminds us that asserting our rights can be an act of obedience.

The gospel does not require our dispossession. It calls us to faithful, informed, courageous engagement for the good of the vulnerable, the flourishing of the church, and the glory of God.

Reflection Questions

1. How has your family of origin, community, or upbringing trained you to "endure"?

2. Are there ways in which your family, community, or upbringing trained you to equate "suffering" with "faithfulness"?

3. Paul leveraged his knowledge of the law to protect himself, his mission, and his community. Do you know the legal rights of citizens, immigrants, and refugees in your country? What steps can you take to better understand them? How can you protect yourself and others with this knowledge?

4. What have you been taught about how the church, at its best, interacts with government? How have you witnessed church–government interactions over the course of your life?

To Endure White Surveillance or Not?

Ashley Boggan

By the 1780s and 1790s, St. George's Methodist Episcopal Church in Philadelphia had become one of the most prominent Methodist congregations in the new republic—and one of its most racially tense. Black Methodists worshipped in growing numbers, drawn by Methodist preaching, discipline, and spiritual vitality. Yet their presence also provoked increasing anxiety among White trustees and leaders, who viewed Black religious gatherings through the lens of control, order, and social hierarchy.

Richard Allen, a licensed Methodist exhorter and preacher, had already demonstrated extraordinary pastoral and organizational gifts. He preached to Black congregants, raised funds, and helped anchor Methodist growth in the city. But as Black attendance increased, so did White surveillance of Black bodies and Black movement within the sanctuary. Trustees began policing where Black worshippers could sit, when they could pray, and how visibly they could participate. What had once been informal segregation hardened into active monitoring.

Allen's own account makes clear that this surveillance was not merely spatial but disciplinary. White leaders feared that autonomous Black religious expression—especially kneeling, praying aloud, or gathering without White oversight—might undermine White authority or suggest spiritual equality. The infamous moment came when Black worshippers, including Absalom Jones, were physically pulled from their knees during prayer and ordered to the gallery. For Allen, this was not simply an insult; it was a theological violation. To interrupt prayer was to deny the legitimacy of Black encounter with God.

In *The Life, Experience, and Gospel Labors of the Rt. Rev. Richard Allen*,[6] Allen describes the event with restraint but unmistakable clarity. He frames the action as coercive, humiliating, and spiritually violent. The issue was not merely seating; it was the insistence that Black devotion must remain invisible, manageable, and subordinate.

Rather than submit to perpetual surveillance, Allen and others made the deliberate decision to leave St. George's. Their exit was an act of theological protest. Allen did not reject Methodism; he rejected White control over Black worship.

EPILOGUE

There Is No Pretty Bow at the End of This Book

Aleze Fulbright and Mike Baughman

Personal Reflection

We write this book with a certain measure of fear and trepidation that comes with vulnerability. We are limited by our time, our context, our experiences, our education, and more. As we are bold enough to evaluate the actions of Paul and other historical figures, we are well aware that future generations (and future versions of ourselves) will likely look back on the words we wrote in 2026 as woefully inadequate. We hope to God they will be. The moral arc of the universe (and of us, as individuals) will bend ever steadily toward justice. We look forward to the day when our words are obsolete.

We are confident that some contemporaries in the church and beyond, who see a more excellent way, will find our perspectives poor, critique our chapters, and wonder why we did not just [fill in the blank]. We hope people will. We do not see this book as a final, definitive word on Paul, equity, or the church. It's our best effort to join a conversation already at work in the twenty-first-century reformation of Christianity in a brave new world.

Public Challenge

If you have reached the end of this book hoping for resolution, clarity, or comfort, we must be honest with you: None is neatly offered here. There is no triumphal conclusion that ties suffering into a redemptive package, making everything feel worth it. There is no assurance that if you do the right thing, things will turn out well. There is no guarantee that faithfulness will be rewarded with safety, affirmation, or institutional approval.

Social action—real social action, not symbolic gestures or carefully curated statements—requires sacrifice; it always has. Civil disobedience, when it is rooted in justice and not ego, is undertaken with the clear expectation of loss. It works by forcing systems of power to reveal themselves. It presses those in authority to either uphold their stated values or punish those who expose the distance between law and righteousness. The problem is that many of us want transformation without consequence. We want prophetic change without personal risk. We want resurrection without crucifixion. But Acts, and particularly the life and witness of Paul, refuses to indulge that fantasy.

Paul does not stumble into conflict with the authorities. He does not misunderstand the risks. He knows exactly what it means to challenge empire, economy, and custom. He understands that preaching a gospel that levels human worth, disrupts exploitative systems, and names Jesus, not Caesar, as Lord will eventually provoke a response. And when that response comes, it is rarely polite. Paul understands something the modern church often forgets: Unjust systems depend on compliance, silence, and invisibility. Civil disobedience interrupts all three; it makes injustice public, and it demands a response that forces the hand of power to either concede or punish, and either outcome reveals the truth. And truth-telling is not accidental but strategic, and it is costly.

We live in a moment where calls for justice are often welcomed only if they remain abstract. We are encouraged to speak in ways that do not inconvenience, disrupt, or unsettle. We are urged to advocate without agitating, to reform without resisting, to love without demanding a cost. Every meaningful movement toward justice has been accompanied by sacrifice. Every expansion of human dignity has been resisted by those who benefit from its restriction. So let us be clear: The call to action at the end of this book is not sentimental; it is a call to risk something real for the sake of God's kin-dom. It is a call to examine what we are willing to lose to tell the truth. To ask whether our theology can survive outside the protection of respectability. To discern when obedience to God will require disobedience to systems that confuse order with justice.

There is no pretty bow because the work is not finished. The reading of Acts does not end with resolution; it ends with Paul under surveillance, preaching anyway. The story stops mid-sentence, as if to say, "Now it is your turn." If this book leaves you unsettled, that is not a failure. It is an invitation. Are you willing to be in the category of "they" and "these people" to be known for the ways you courageously moved forward in ways that turn the world upside down for the greater good of all?

Reflection Questions

1. What emotions surfaced for you as you read the epilogue (discomfort, conviction, resistance, clarity, grief, excitement, resolve)? What might those emotions be teaching you, and what will you do with the learning?

2. Paul submits himself to legal authorities at great personal cost, not because the system is just but because his personal cost exposes injustice. Where might obedience to God require you to risk consequence and not retreat into protection?

3. What forms of privilege (legal, social, economic, geographic, institutional, or other) do you carry? How might God be inviting you to leverage or relinquish them for the sake of others?

4. Civil disobedience assumes loss. What losses feel most threatening to you right now (reputation, security, relationships, access, belonging)? How do those fears shape your choices and your next most faithful steps?

5. The Book of Acts ends without resolution. This book does the same. What unfinished work is God placing before you, not as an idea but as a concrete next step after reading this book?

Notes

Chapter 1

1 Willie James Jennings, *The Christian Imagination: Theology and the Origins of Race* (Yale University Press, 2010).

2 Michelle Alexander, *The New Jim Crow* (New Press, 2010).

3 Elisabeth Schüssler Fiorenza, *In Memory of Her* (Crossroad, 1983).

4 For more on John Wesley's childhood and theological development, see Richard Heitzenrater, *Wesley and the People Called Methodist*, 2nd ed. (Abingdon Press, 2013). See also Henry D. Rack, *Reasonable Enthusiast: John Wesley and the Rise of Methodism*, 3rd ed. (Epworth Press, 2002).

5 John Wesley, "Letter," *Arminian Magazine*, April 1790.

Chapter 2

1 Sarah Kay, "If I Should Have a Daughter…" TED Talk, March 2011, https://www.ted.com/talks/sarah_kay_if_i_should_have_a_daughter.

2 "Baptismal Covenant I." *The United Methodist Book of Worship*, ed. Andy Langford (The United Methodist Publishing House, 1992), 88.

3 "Baptismal Covenant I," 88.

4 Nel Irvin Painter, *Sojourner Truth: A Life, A Symbol* (WW Norton & Co., 1997); Sojourner Truth, *Narrative of Sojourner Truth* (Penguin Classics, 1998).

5 From an untitled speech delivered at the Women's Convention, Akron, Ohio, 1851.

Chapter 3

1 *Book of Common Prayer* (Church of England, 1662).

2 "A Service of Word and Table I and Introductions to the Other Forms," *The United Methodist Book of Worship*, ed. Andy Langford (The United Methodist Publishing House, 1992), 8.

3 Donald G. Mathews, "The Women Delegates of 1888," in *Religion in the Old South* (University of Chicago Press, 1977).

4 *Minutes of the General Conference of the Methodist Episcopal Church, 1888* (Hunt & Eaton, 1888).

5 *Minutes of the General Conference.*

6 *Minutes of the General Conference.*

Chapter 4

1 "Baptismal Covenant I," 88.

2 Rack, *Reasonable Enthusiast; John Wesley, Journal and Diaries*, vol. 19, *The Works of John Wesley* (Abingdon Press, 1990).

3 Wesley, *Journal and Diaries*, vol. 19.

4 Charles Wesley, *The Manuscript Journal of Charles Wesley*, ed. S.T. Kimbrough Jr. (Kingswood Books, 2007).

5 Wesley, *Journal and Diaries*, vol. 19.

Chapter 5

1 Wayne A. Meeks, *The First Urban Christians* (Yale University Press, 1983), 51–54.

2 John K. Chow, *Patronage and Power* (JSOT Press, 1992), 85–90.

3 See, for example, Frank A. Thomas, *Surviving a Dangerous Sermon* (Abingdon Press, 2020).

4 Albert J. Raboteau, *Slave Religion* (Oxford University Press, 1978), 212–220.

5 Richard Allen, *The Life, Experience, and Gospel Labors of the Rt. Rev. Richard Allen* (Martin & Boden, 1833).

6 Christopher H. Evans, *The Social Gospel in American Religion* (NYU Press, 2017).

7 Boyd Stanley Schlenther, *Queen of the Methodists: The Countess of Huntingdon and the Eighteenth-Century Crisis of Faith and Society* (Durham Academic Press, 1997).

8 Selina Hastings, Countess of Huntingdon, "Letter to Charles Wesley, June 7, 1749," in *The Letters of the Rev. John Wesley*, ed. John Telford (Epworth Press, 1931).

9 Luke Tyerman, *The Life and Times of the Countess of Huntingdon*, 2 vols. (Hodder & Stoughton, 1870); Boyd Stanley Schlenther, *Queen of the Methodists: The Countess of Huntingdon and the Eighteenth-Century Crisis of Faith and Society* (Durham Academic Press, 1997).

Chapter 6

1 James Davison Hunter, *To Change the World: The Irony, Tragedy, and Possibility of Christianity in the Late Modern World* (Oxford University Press, 2010), 96.

2 Jemar Tisby, *The Color of Compromise: The Truth About the American Church's Complicity in Racism* (Zondervan, 2019), 15.

3 Michael Lipka, "Why America's 'Nones' Left Religion Behind," Pew Research Center, August 24, 2016, https://www.pewresearch.org/short-reads/2016/08/24/why-americas-nones-left-religion-behind/.

4 Kristin Kobes Du Mez, *Jesus and John Wayne* (Liveright, 2020), 12–14.

5 Willie James Jennings, *After Whiteness: An Education in Belonging* (Eerdmans, 2020), 7.

6 John D'Emilio, *Sexual Politics, Sexual Communities: The Making of a Homosexual Minority in the United States, 1940–1970*, 2nd ed. (University of Chicago Press, 1998); Ashley Boggan, *Entangled: A History of American Methodism, Politics, and Sexuality* (Abingdon Press, 2025).

Chapter 7

1 John Wesley, *Sermon 111 On the Omnipresence of God. III.1*, https://wesley.nnu.edu/john-wesley/the-sermons-of-john-wesley-1872-edition/sermon-111-on-the-omnipresence-of-god/.

2 Brooklyn Moore, "A Texas Dad Rose to TikTok Fame Reviewing Restaurants in the Most Texas Dad Way," *Texas Monthly*, November 18, 2025, https://www.texasmonthly.com/food/dine-with-kent-tik-tok/.

3 Nathan Bangs, *A History of the Methodist Episcopal Church*, 4 vols. (Carlton & Phillips, 1857); James B. Finley, *History of the Wyandott Mission at Upper Sandusky, Ohio* (J. F. Wright & L. Swormstedt, 1840); J. M. Peck, *Life and Times of Rev. John Stewart, the First Missionary to the Wyandotts* (Methodist Book Concern, 1865).

Chapter 8

1 James H. Cone, *The Cross and the Lynching Tree* (Orbis Books, 2011).

2 Frederick Douglass, *Narrative of the Life of Frederick Douglass, an American Slave* (Anti-Slavery Office, 1845).

3 Fannie Lou Hamer, "I'm Sick and Tired of Being Sick and Tired," speech delivered at the Williams Institutional CME Church, Harlem, New York, December 20, 1964.

4 *The Booke of Discipline of The United Methodist Church* (The United Methodist Publishing House, 1984), ¶304.3.

5 Andrew K. T. Yip, *The Politics of Counter-Rejection: Gay Christians and the Church* (Ashgate, 2003); Beth Stroud, "A Pastoral Response to the Church Trial," in *Love Your Neighbor: The Reconciliation Movement in the United Methodist Church*, ed. Thomas Frank (Abingdon Press, 2014).

6 "Defrocked Pastor Beth Stroud Reinstated After Policy Change," United Methodist News Service, May 2024.

7 Jimmy Creech, *Adam's Gift: A Memoir of a Pastor's Calling to Defy the Church's Persecution of Lesbians and Gays* (Duke University Press, 2011).

8 "Defrocked Pastor Beth Stroud Reinstated."

Chapter 9

1 Henry Boehm, *Reminiscences, Historical and Biographical, of Sixty-Four Years in the Ministry*, ed. Joseph B. Wakeley (Carlton & Porter, 1865), 157.

2 Gregory S. Lampe, "Harry Hosier: Black Preacher Extraordinary," *Methodist History* 45, no. 2 (January 2007): 74–89.

3 Francis Asbury, *The Journal and Letters of Francis Asbury*, vol. 1, ed. Elmer T. Clark et al. (Abingdon, 1958), 364.

4 Asbury, *The Journal of the Rev. Francis Asbury*, 328.

5 Asbury, *Journal and Letters*, 1:366.

6 J. B. Wakeley, *The Patriarch of One Hundred Years: Reminiscences of Rev. Henry Boehm* (Nelson & Phillips, 1875), 90–91.

7 Thomas Coke, *Journal of the Rev. Dr. Thomas Coke* (J. Paramore, 1816), 76.

8 Thomas Coke, *Extracts of the Journals of the Late Rev. Thomas Coke* (J. Paramore, 1816), 61.

Chapter 10

1 Heidi Schlumpf, "Faith Leaders Face Prosecution for Migrant Ministry," *National Catholic Reporter*, January 25, 2019.

2 James B. McPherson, "Humanitarian Aid Workers Under Federal Scrutiny," *New York Times*, 2019.

3 Peter Smith, "Cities Use Zoning Laws to Shut Down Church Homeless Ministries," Associated Press, 2020.

4 Katherine Stewart, *The Power Worshippers* (Bloomsbury, 2020).

5 Evelyn Brooks Higginbotham, *Righteous Discontent* (Harvard University Press, 1993).

6 Richard Allen, *The Life, Experience, and Gospel Labours of the Rt. Rev. Richard Allen, to Which Is Annexed the Rise and Progress of the African Methodist Episcopal Church in the United States of America* (Martin & Boden, 1833).